CASE WORK IN PREACHING

CASE WORK IN PREACHING

By
EZRA RHOADES, D.D.

NEW YORK
Fleming H. Revell Company
LONDON AND EDINBURGH

New York: 158 Fifth Avenue
London: 99 Anerley Road

PREFACE

It is believed that this book is radically different from any previously published.

For Whom?

It is contributed respectfully and fraternally to those American preachers (a vast majority) who feel doubtful and uncomfortable about their own pulpit work.

By Whom?

The author is a man who, after teaching many classes of divinity students and after listening to hundreds of preachers in America and other lands, believes that the usefulness of most ministers could be multiplied if they would acknowledge and eliminate apparently trivial errors, eccentricities and inhibitions.

Why?

Because most ministers, dissatisfied with their own preaching, experience not only " blue Mondays " but blue Sundays and, possibly, seven blue days a week.

Because they feel that their seminary courses in homiletics were fragmentary and inadequate, much less thorough than the training given to lawyers, doctors, or even skilled mechanics.

Because they wish that they could have the benefit of sympathetic and understanding criticism.

Because they know that what may seem but minor faults may result in major failures.

Because they plainly see that the Christian Church today is in tragic need of the most powerful preaching that possibly can be given.

What is the Plan?

The semi-fiction behind this work is that a professor

of homiletics receives from former students a large number of requests for postgraduate counsel. He loves those young apostles and he tries to comply, not cruelly but with enough frankness to make his advice genuinely useful.

Some of the faults indicated, common throughout the Church, may be the very ones that are retarding the progress of the readers.

Each chapter is followed by pages strictly private. These are to be used following and preceding earnest prayer, which may be in the words of the reader, of the author, or of both. The questions should be answered with the utmost sincerity and after searching self-examination. The replies, presumably written with pencil, should be positively for no eyes but those of the minister himself. Revisions should be made from time to time as the chapters receive repeated attention. Manifestly, the entries of supreme importance should be those following the questions, " What ought I to do? " and " What *will* I do? "

The author himself is using the book, glad to be spurred constantly to seek higher efficiency for the Kingdom.

It has been gratifying to receive from leading ministers of many denominations testimony that, having read the manuscript, they too have been roused to more careful effort and have been helped to attain their potential usefulness and joy.

One criterion of homiletic excellence ought always to be borne in mind. The best sermon need not necessarily be the one that is most eloquent or the one that is most scholarly or the one that most closely follows the class-room rules. Always the best sermon is *the one that does the most good*. The realization of that truth, seemingly so obvious as to make its statement almost ridiculous, would transform for the better the work of many a Christian preacher.

E. R.

CONTENTS

EXCELSIOR, PLEASE GOD!

(Rev. Dan M. Hathaway and other former students having asked a divinity school professor for postgraduate
criticisms, he takes them at their word, and, in the spirit of
an affectionate older brother, makes a few suggestions
that, even if painful, ought to be helpful.)

DOCTOR RAYMOND, of blessed memory, taught the
same subject in divinity school for over thirty-five years
and yet his courses never became stale or stereotyped.
Always his students issued from class with smiling faces
and with a sense of being fed and uplifted. " How is it,
Doctor," I asked him, " that you can keep your work so
fresh and fine? " He opened his notebook, drew out a
folded slip and allowed me to read his perpetual slogan:
" Every year every lesson in every course at least a little
better."

CASE I

Shall I Really Tell You?

Classroom Number 6

Rev. Dan M. Hathaway,
Millford, Vermont.

My dear Dan:

Do you mean it? Honest Injun?

I have received your package of sermons, being greatly
honored to have you and the other fine fellows turn to
me for criticism and counsel. I am willing to put in a
great deal of time for your benefit, but before I begin I

9

want to be entirely certain about your attitude. Do you and Frank and Robert really want me to be candid enough to be of some important service? Are you thick-skinned or thin-skinned?

It takes grace ninety-nine and forty-four one-hundredths pure to accept criticism in the Christian spirit and to use it properly in our apostolic development.

I have had some recent experience in this matter that makes me a little wary and hesitant. A former student, not of your group or acquaintance, appealed to me much as you men are doing. He said that he knew that he had many faults as a preacher. In that he was correct. He said that he wanted to have them pointed out so that he could overcome them. In that, as I discovered, he was mistaken.

I wrote to him in a gentle, fraternal spirit, suggesting a few of his outstanding errors. His grammar would have disgraced a boy of the eighth grade. Split infinitives! I am no purist in regard to that detail; but this fellow placed his preposition beyond even telescopic vision of his verb! He confused numbers. He mixed metaphors. Beginning with grammar and rhetoric, he gave horrible examples of about every homiletical sin that you could imagine.

I took him at his word and wrote to him kindly but frankly. What response do you suppose he made? Did he send a letter of humble gratitude? He did not. Did he present a Thanksgiving turkey as a slight token of appreciation? He did not.

He was thoroughly *mad*. He was foolish enough to write and mail a letter while he was still smarting under the sense of insult and injury. The burden of his communication was that I had many, many faults of my own (alas, too true), that I was a petty crank regarding some of my own little whims, that I didn't know a good thing when I saw it, that I had better mind my own business, and so forth and so forth. You see, he had desired, not honest criticism, but praise. When I met him at a convention not long after he seemed as cold as a polar bear.

He was more sensitive than sensible. If I thought that you and your fellow-requesters were of that spirit I wouldn't waste one minute reading your manuscripts.

Here are several points to be accepted in all sincerity by every applicant for helpful criticism:

1. Preaching is very difficult and in modern days is becoming more and more difficult.

2. With all my scholastic training my preparation has been sadly inadequate.

3. I am not perfect in my pulpit work.

4. I must try to find out how others see me, so that I may rightly evaluate my own work and know where to strengthen my efforts.

5. I must not be offended if some of the criticisms cut very deep in very tender flesh.

6. I must not retort, either in words or thought, that my critic has the same faults that he mentions or others just as bad.

7. I must show my appreciation by trying to carry out the suggestions offered by my mentor.

Dan, I think that we ministers are in danger of being spoiled by the indiscriminate praise of kindly deacons, sweet mothers in Israel and admiring young ladies. We often need to have our intellectual ears soundly boxed.

In other walks in life workers are helped by plain speaking and sometimes by brutal speaking. I know a lad who is apprentice to a high-class printer. He is going to be a high-class printer himself, but there are days when he doesn't think so. During his first year he went home so stung by the relentless call-downs of his boss that he was ready to throw up his job. He hated his employer. Now, however, he knows that every word, apparently cruel, is uttered for his own good and he thinks that Mr. X. is one of the saints of the earth.

As you know, Doctor Z——— is one of the most expert

brain surgeons in this metropolis, and, for that matter, in America. No one can estimate the number of lives which his tender fingers have saved from disaster. He has the reputation, however, of being "hard-boiled" and even violent with his nurses and assistant doctors. He demands best efforts from every associate and unless that "best" is exceedingly good he has a change in his staff. His language in the operating room is not polite but it is understandable and effective. What is the result? Competent nurses and doctors. Those who have backbone enough to endure his criticism and sense enough to appreciate its spirit and value come through with marvellous efficiency. How do you think our young ministers would like to serve under some leader who was as merciless as Doctor Z———?

Old Colonel R———, of Burlingham, was a terror and a nuisance for settled pastors and also for visiting preachers. Every Sunday he sat in a front pew, pencil in hand, and made a note of every slip in grammar or pronunciation. Before leaving the church he would very dutifully present his list of criticisms to the squirming Chrysostom. A certain new minister stood that procedure for a couple of months and then, tired and nervous, indulged in a regrettable brain storm. One Sunday he seized the Colonel's papers, tore them to shreds and ordered the astonished old gentleman to go home and stay there. The next day, however, deeply repentant, he apologized and besought a continuance of the suggestions. Today that preacher stands high on the list of Christian leaders, and he says that Colonel R——— deserves half the credit. He did "frae monie a blunder free him, and foolish notion."

Just write to me again, dear Dan. If you say, "Go ahead, Doctor," I'll proceed in real earnest and fear not.

Yours with unremitting affection,

The Pedagogue Homiletical.

CASE II

Phillips Brooks Did

Dear Morgan:

When Phillips Brooks was rector of Trinity Church in Boston and was acclaimed as one of the world's greatest preachers he continued to take lessons in homiletics. Not believing himself to have mastered the apostolic art, he went in all humility to a teacher in a small divinity school in his neighborhood and sought criticism and suggestion. As a matter of fact, other leading ministers in the vicinity, some of them of international reputation, had their special private instructions from this same mentor. No great preacher himself, this man had a wide reputation as a homiletical helper and he had the privilege and honor of increasing the power and usefulness of some of the greatest speakers of all time.

Have you ever thought of taking postgraduate courses in pulpit work? Why not? I know that you take them in Bible study, in ethics, in sociology, in comparative religion. Good. But why not in the particular subject upon which your life usefulness very largely depends? You are near enough to a theological school to arrange courses with some competent professor. Not of your denomination? What of that? Very likely you would find that fact broadening and altogether advantageous. Go with open mind, Morgan, dig into the work as you would with any other difficult course. Demand progress, as even Brooks demanded progress.

This same suggestion I am making to several of the boys who have written to me for help about their sermons.

CASE III

Pew Number 94

Dear Wallace:

You say that you wish I could sit in your congregation every Sunday. Thank you. I would enjoy it and I hope that we would continue to be good friends.

But who is that regular attendant, there in the fifth seat from the left side? Fine-looking young lady, evidently educated and intellectually alert. Very attentive to every sermon, isn't she? Your wife? I thought so. Why not accept *her* as your counsellor, inasmuch as she is always with you and is a very competent person?

I still have the letter that you wrote to me at the time of your wedding. You said:

" She is mine own; and I as rich in having such a treasure
As twenty seas if all their isles were pearl,
Their waters nectar and their rocks pure gold."

I don't think that you overestimated her worth.

She wants to help you. Of course she does. Her success in life depends largely upon your own. Moreover, as a Christian woman, she is eager to have you accomplish your maximum possible usefulness.

Is she helping you as much as possible?

Some ministers simply build bars between themselves and their wives when it comes to criticism. They are irritable and resentful if the good women venture any suggestion that their pulpit work is not a hundred per cent perfect. One parsoness said, " I'd like to tell Frank a few things but the moment I begin on that line he gets a sick headache."

The other day at the University we had a visiting lecturer of international eminence. Oh dear, I wish his wife had told him not to make himself ridiculous in the management of his glasses. They were small rimless glasses, attached to his waistcoat by a wide ribbon. He didn't use them to read with at all, but continually put them on and took them off. How many times in the course of an hour? I don't know. One of the boys said that he counted up to a thousand times and then got tired of watching. Some of the young folks giggled and some of the old folks fidgeted.

I am not going to emphasize your particular faults at this time, but only emphasize the fact that your wife ought to tell you about some little things of large importance. Do you constantly button and unbutton your coat? Do you throw your arms about without significance? Do you repeatedly sip water? Do you stand in the pulpit with your hands in your pockets? Do you make senseless facial contortions? Do you lean too far forward? Do you lean too far backward?

Then, as to diction, enunciation, pronunciation, good taste, and so forth and so forth—your fine wife, a college graduate and a former teacher, is well able to be your helpful partner.

Are you afraid that I am suggesting something that may break up your family? God give that woman wisdom to present her criticisms so kindly and tactfully that they will help and not hurt! God give you grace to be so anxious for service that you will accept every word in the spirit with which it is spoken!

Wallace, dear fellow, solicit full co-operation from the girl in Pew 94.

CASE IV

"Is That Me?"

Dear Edgar:

A prominent actress recently attended a preview of a new picture, and, seeing herself as others were to see her, was distressed and incredulous. " Oh golly," she cried, " is *that* me? "

There is a young lady named Mrs. Edgar Matheson who possesses a full-length mirror. Inasmuch as she is not always surveying herself or her gowns, can you not make use of it once in a while?

I have often thought that it would be a good thing for every minister to have an ample looking-glass as part of his personal equipment. He ought not to spend much time before it. He might get vain if he were a modern Apollo, or, if he were like most of us, he might get downhearted. Speaking seriously, occasional use of the mirror for sermonic rehearsal ought to be enlightening and helpful.

I do not advise you, Edgar, to practice every sermon before a glass, or to practice any one repeatedly. That might lead to self-consciousness, lack of spontaneity, affectation. Once in a while, however, the mirror might help you to detect and overcome some awkward position, some insignificant gesture, some irrelevant and distracting facial expression.

CASE V

Beatrice Showed Me Your Books

Dear Douglas:

In due course of time I will study (D. V.) your submitted manuscripts. Please don't hurry me. So many of you boys have concentrated on me at once that it will be several months before I can attend to you all.

I am moved, however, to say a few things to you before I even look at your sermons. I have seen your library. You will remember that one day as I was passing through Farley I dropped in at your parsonage and made a little call. While I was waiting for you to return from a wedding your sister Beatrice took me into your library and told me to make myself at home.

What a wonderful collection you are making! Fine books! Classics and others that will become classics! I congratulate you upon your volumes on the Bible, on social problems, on religious questions, on general literature. Keep on. You are investing wisely—especially if you continue to open the books that you buy.

After all, however, your library seems to be strangely out of balance for a Christian preacher. Where are your books on homiletics?

When I visit a lawyer, I find many volumes dealing with the practical details of his own profession. When I visit a doctor, I find whole rows of books in regard to the latest medical discoveries and methods. These men, as a matter of course, are carrying on postgraduate study in their own homes. If they fail to keep up with the times they may as well take down their shingles.

Your library has no section on the art of making sermons. I did find a copy of Phelps on *The Theory of Preaching,* a very good book, albeit it was written before your father was born. Why not have a whole shelf of well-studied works on homiletical practice?

There are plenty of them. Excellent ones are coming out every year, as you will see if you read the catalogues and the magazine advertisements. Last month, for instance, I bought *The Miracle of Preaching* by Park and *The Preparation and Delivery of Sermons* by Patton.

The sale for such potentially helpful books is exceedingly small, which indicates that your shortsightedness is only one instance of a common ministerial unwisdom.

It does seem strange that American clergymen, oppressed by the magnitude of their tasks and depressed by shrinking congregations, are not eager to read every word that might help them to pulpit efficiency.

I shall never forget the inspiration and the practical assistance that I gained many years ago from Beecher's

Yale Lectures on Preaching and from Nathaniel J. Burton's *Yale Lectures*. I am still reading all such books that I can get my hands on. And every one teaches me something about my very difficult art.

You ask my criticism. First of all, I criticize you for your evident neglect of strictly professional reading.

CASE VI

Visiting Around

Dear Claude:

You seem to be profoundly dissatisfied with C. R. H. That is all right if you don't carry your humility beyond the danger point. I think that you are quite a man in spite of your self-depreciation and so do the other members of our faculty; but, of course, we agree with you that there is room for improvement.

Have you ever thought of " visiting around," with the hope of finding out how other men do the job that you find so difficult?

The farmers in our neighborhood used to do something similar to that. They taught each other a good many things, Luke swapping ideas with Eben and David swapping ideas with 'Lisha. That was one reason that we made such a fine record at the Cattle Show.

I think that you could visit the ministers right in your own community, the hope being that by exchanging counsel you all could become more efficient. From even the least brother in your town you probably could derive something helpful. And in all likelihood there is with you some good father in Christ who could give you younger men a great many helpful hints. It was said of one dear man in Massachusetts that no preacher ever settled in the town with him without becoming a better preacher because of the fellowship.

Then you have ministers of your own denomination not a thousand miles away. Why not call on one of them once in a while with the express purpose of a homiletical conference? It was a great day for your friend Hammond when Dubois explained to him the use of different colored pencils in keeping his outlines clearly in mind. Conversely, it was a great day for Dubois when Hammond suggested the use of the various Biblical translations.

Besides consulting other ministers in their studies, you ought to hear them preach. You can do that at union services and at conventions. And you may think it wise to follow the example of Doctor McRobbins, who used to deny himself certain books and use the money that he saved for Sunday morning trips to other churches. Presumably you can get a supply for an occasional service.

When you do hear a brother preach you will find, no matter how eminent he may be, that he has both weakness and strength. When you detect something that detracts you may say, " Alas, I have been doing that very thing myself—but nevermore! " And when you notice something that helps along you may inquire whether or not you, even with your different personality and location, may not, without deadly imitation, follow his example.

PRAYER TO PRECEDE SELF-EXAMINATION

God of all truth, I thank Thee that Thou hast commissioned and challenged me as a servant and as a spokesman.

Rescue me, I pray, from both vanity and defeatism.

Because I am unspeakably grateful for the opportunity to work in Thy Kingdom may I insist upon making every day a better day.

Help me to banish all vainglory and all selfishness from my ministry and, because of utter consecration, to keep progressive in usefulness.

SEARCHING SELF-EXAMINATION

(These questions are for no eyes but those of the minister himself. Each is to be considered thoughtfully, prayerfully and repeatedly.)

1. Do I frequently pause in my busy career and impress upon myself the dignity and privilege of Christian apostleship?

   Answer ....

2. Do I constantly emphasize the ideal of progress in my homiletical work?

   Answer ....

3. Am I properly repentant for having failed sometimes to insist upon my best possible work?

   Answer ....

4. Do I allow excessive humility to discourage and paralyze me?

   Answer ....

5. Or do

   > " I hold it truth, with him who sings
   >   To one clear harp in divers tones,
   >   That men may rise on stepping stones
   >   Of their dead selves to higher things "?

   Answer ....

6. Have I in the past year overcome any important fault?

   Answer ....

7. Have I in the past year acquired any important skills or techniques?

   Answer ....

8. Did I receive at college a good introduction to the study of homiletics?

   Answer ....

9. Does criticism, even when well intended, give me a head-ache and " take the starch out of me "?

   Answer ....

10. Does it make me grouchy?

   Answer ....

11. Do I get as much helpful criticism as I should from the members of my family?

   Answer ....

12. Do I seek suggestions from the wise and cultured members of my parish?

   Answer ....

13. Am I willing to work for self-development as hard as a doctor or a lawyer must?

   Answer ....

14. Do I study books on the art of homiletics?

   Answer ....

15. Do I study preachers' magazines?

   Answer ....

16. Do I sometimes rehearse before a mirror?

   Answer ....

17. Do I learn as much as I ought from other preachers?

   Answer ....

18. Do I properly consider the possibility of postgraduate courses in homiletics?

   Answer ....

19. Do I pray as I should before composing a sermon?

   Answer ....

20. Do I pray as I should before entering my pulpit?

Answer ....

After considering all the suggested points, what ought I to do?

What *will* I do?

Prayer: I thank Thee, gracious Father, for new inspira-
tion, new vision, new power to do Thy will.

SECTION TWO

"WHO BEARETH GLAD TIDINGS"

(It being apparent that some young ministers whom he has trained, including Rev. Jeremiah Strong, are neither feeling nor conveying the supreme joy of the Christian message, the professor urges them to cheer up and to cheer up their parishioners.)

IT was the custom of Walt Whitman to give "three cheers for the universe." It was hardly necessary for him to do it orally, for anybody who met him anywhere could read on his face and in his carriage the fact of his enthusiasm, his joy and his gratitude. So it was when he was wandering in poverty; so it was when he was ministering in the dreadful army hospitals; so it was when, in old age, he sat day after day in an invalid's chair. There have been Christian ministers who have given evidence of applauding the cosmos as persistently

as did " the good, gray poet." Why not all apostles of
" the glorious gospel of the blessed God " ?

CASE I

A Frowning Evangel

Classroom Number 6

Rev. Jeremiah Strong,
Bristol, Oregon.

My dear Jeremiah:
Few men can be scolded into the Kingdom of God.
Few can be howled in or growled in. The common scold
is not an inspiring or efficient leader in the home, in the
church or anywhere else. You have known cases of
harassed, overworked, under-appreciated women who
have degenerated from faultfinders to shrews and from
shrews to veritable Xantippes. Alas for them and for
their unfortunate families! You, a Christian minister,
are supposed to be an expert in the art of persuasion and
you ought to know better than to indulge in constant,
carping criticism.

In this letter I am not going to be so inconsistent as to
scold you. I shall write with a persistent smile, being
truly your friend; but, being truly your friend, I shall
speak with entire frankness.

Your six sermons, powerful in many ways, are made
impotent by tiresome bitterness and petulance. It is not
strange that your congregations are infinitesimal. Have
you never heard of the old, old proverb that you can
catch more flies with honey than with vinegar?

When you were in school you were critical and hyper-
critical. If anything or anybody were right, you certainly never found it out. I remember your censorious

attitude in chapel talks and Thelomathesian addresses as well as in ordinary conversation, and it was not such as to result in either popularity or usefulness.

I had hoped that with a few years of experience among heartsick men and women you would reform your thought and your speech, but these manuscripts show that you have gone from bad to very bad. Your people are condemned in unmeasured terms for parochial parsimony, for absence from church functions, for failure to go to the polls, for lack of interest in religious education, for gossip, for neglect of the Bible, for bridge playing, for thoughtlessness about parsonage repairs, for movie madness, and so on and on. All in six short sermons! What can you find to growl about for a whole year?

Here in one discourse you fiercely berate the wives and mothers of the present generation, unmercifully condemning their slovenly housekeeping, their careless cooking, their incompetent discipline. Is it not barely possible that you would accomplish more good by setting up a few shining examples of women who have seen their opportunities as parents and home-makers and by fidelity to simple duties have made their lives sublime?

You have sent me a sermon on gossip from the text, " Thou shalt not bear false witness against thy neighbor." Every hearer certainly knew what you meant— and probably *whom* you meant. I suggest that you preach a different message, one on " A Consecrated Tongue," containing no harsh criticism of anybody, but suggesting how a life may, by wholesome, kindly, helpful speech, be made beautiful and truly useful.

Here is your sermon on " Faith and Finance." It is well written as far as English goes—you always have had an unusual facility in the use of language. You are quite unsparing, however, when you speak of those who spend money for gum, cosmetics, tobacco, gasoline and movies. When you wrote that sermon you intended to hit some people and to hit them hard. You thought that they would squirm down there in the pews. All right. Probably they did. But are you certain that such tactics win to willing sacrifice and a keener love for the Kingdom? Suppose you get for yourself the reputation of a crank, a kill-joy and a crosspatch—will that help the cause that you have at heart? I have heard of ministers who have always been demanding, demanding, demanding, money and more money. Usually they have had short pastorates and little financial success. How would it do to try a different approach? Suppose you should emphasize for a little while the beauty of sacrifice, the privilege of giving for God, the glory of partnership with Him? That would be more dignified, wouldn't it? I am inclined to think that it would be more fruitful.

No one can deny that there are times when congregations need some " good plain talk." I would be the last to advocate that you should always make yourself " just too sweet for anything." But the times for tongue-lashing are comparatively rare. You must not forget that by constant dwelling on the sins and deficiencies of your people you make yourself not only disagreeable, but sadly ineffective.

Spurgeon, prince of preachers, used to emphasize the " wooing " element in good pulpit work. In many a sermon he wooed his listeners with the tenderness of a great lover and the gladness of a glowing evangelist, and his persuasion left every hearer with an intense resolution to seek the truth and to be true to the truth and faithful to the faith.

I wish you would read Isaiah 38: 17, " In love to my soul thou hast delivered it from the pit of corruption." In another translation the passage is, " Thou hast loved me from the pit." Don't you think that your pulpit work would be more welcome and more effective if you would introduce the love element into it? Read once in a while Goldsmith's description of the grand old village preacher:

> " And as a bird each fond endearment tries
> To tempt its new-fledged offspring to the skies,
> He tried each art, reproved each dull delay,
> Allur'd to brighter worlds and led the way."

Try a little endearment, Jeremiah. Allure a little more; resent and threaten a little less. For every time you preach against something that is wrong, preach five times in favor of something that is beautiful and fine and noble and Christian. Greatly recommend the fruits of the spirit, which are " love, joy, peace, longsuffering, gentleness, goodness, faith, meekness, temperance." Young man, with your fervent spirit and with your many excellencies, you ought to have a magnetic ministry, rich in blessing for yourself and your people.

The supreme assurance in St. John's Gospel is that Jesus, being lifted up, will draw all men unto Him. Notice that He is not to *drive* them with rebuke and threat; He is to *draw* them by His demonstration of a love that never faileth.

Yours for the " glorious good news,"

The Pedagogue Homiletical.

CASE II

Vanity of Vanities

Dear Elton:

You did it. I didn't believe that you would, but you did.

In theological school, when you were blue enough to sell indigo by the carload, you wrote a doleful homily on the text of depression, " Vanity of vanities, all is vanity." You preached it before your fellow students, assuring them of the futility of all human effort and, presumably, of divine effort as well. We all thought that your digestion was at fault and in our criticisms advised you to take a spring tonic. It never occurred to us that your melancholia was to become chronic, especially as outside of the pulpit you always seemed to be one of the jolliest of the jolly.

I had been astonished to hear that you had preached that same sermon in your parish and in other places where you had been for exchange. It must have been one of your favorites.

And then at Dixon! You were invited to address three hundred young people, including a wonderful group of college students. What an opportunity to uplift them and inspire them to noble and aggressive Christian living! McPherson told me that you were intending to give that same old dissertation of despair. I wouldn't believe him. But you did it! I sat in the back seat, groaning in spirit.

In this batch of submitted sermons I find the same general attitude manifested throughout. The "vanity" text might have fitted any one of them. Elton, what *is* the matter? Life hasn't used you with constant cruelty. You have a good body. You are married to a beautiful and gifted young girl. People treat you kindly. You have received the Christian good news. Except for your homiletics, you give no evidence of pessimism.

I urge you to alter your sermonic attitude while you are young and before you have contracted unbreakable habits of gloom. Put some smiles into your discourses. Emphasize the joys of Jesus. Convince your people of the infinite love that is at the heart of the universe. Give them something to be courageous about. Send them away from every service with new hope and new determination.

Elton, how can you expect to win people to Heaven if the corners of your mouth point in exactly the opposite direction?

CASE III

Atrabilious

Dear Guy:

You are to be congratulated upon the scholarship indicated by your sermons, but you are not to be congratulated upon the philosophy of life.

What do you really believe about the universe in which you are privileged (or compelled) to exist? Is it a failure or is it a success? Is it God-deserted or is it God-filled?

I am going to confide something to you. One of your very loyal and helpful parishioners was speaking about you the other day. " Yes," he said, " our Guy is a fine fellow in many ways, but I am sorry to say that he is atrabilious." I nodded wisely, just as though I knew what the word meant, and said, " Oh, isn't it too bad! " When I got home I ran to my unabridged and found the definition. Of course, you know it.

If you are atrabilious, I'll tell you what I think you ought to do. You ought to mourn less and pray more. You ought to cultivate the habit of thanksgiving in your private devotions, just listing a hundred or so of the million reasons you have for gratitude. Do you always pray before you compose? I don't see how you can be quite so melancholy if you do. Give thanks that you are an accepted apostle of the Most High and give enthusiastic thanks that you have a message of beauty, of hope, of deliverance, of salvation. Then I think that neither you nor your sermons will be quite so atrabilious.

CASE IV

A Taste in the Mouth

Dear Warren:

A parishioner of Frederick W. Robertson said, " I love our preacher because he always leaves me with such a pleasant taste in the mouth." That was a long time ago, but I suppose that churchgoing men and women, weary, perplexed, hard-pressed in a hundred ways, still long for such pulpit messages as will leave them with a pleasant taste.

Of the six sermons that you sent last week, I think that two would send the people home with some new inspiration, hope, spiritual power. Hearers would be uplifted and helped by your excellent discourses on " Hope Thou in God " and " The Better Way and the Better Day." I would be, and the " professoress," who has read all your manuscripts, says that she would be.

The other four sermons, however, are destructive rather than constructive, denunciatory rather than uplifting. Have you thought this matter over? Is it better to call people down or to call them *up?* Robertson was no namby-pamby preacher. He did not avoid difficult subjects and he did not encourage sin or thoughtlessness. The point is that he had the tact to leave his people always with some added " enthusiasm for man," some nobler conception of self, some fuller confidence in a saving God. I wish you could develop the Robertsonian attitude.

CASE V

Noblesse Oblige

Dear Calvin:

Grammar: 100. Rhetoric: 100. Construction: 100. Joy: 50.

That is about the grading that I could give on your sample sermons. You expected me to criticize on grammar, rhetoric and construction; but on all those points you are exceptionally strong. I miss something, however, something unspeakably important. I miss the supreme *gladness* that ought to characterize a Christian sermon.

You are not like one of your classmates, who seems to preach nothing but wickedness and woe; yet a professor would have to be in a liberal mood who could give you a grade of 50 on joy.

You *are* glad, are you not? You fall asleep every night with a smile, do you not? You awake with a song in your heart, do you not? I assume that you give thanks every hour for the privilege of being in God's world and in God's work. I assume that your whole intellectual and spiritual life is filled with thanksgiving that you have the revelation of a loving God, of a competent Christ and of a successful universe.

Your duty is to impart something of your own happiness to your people, to give them the Gospel in such measure that, in spite of pain, sorrow and disappointment, they will live conqueringly, helpfully, happily.

You know the old motto, *Noblesse oblige.* You remember the text, " Unto whomsoever much is given of him much also shall be required."

I would like to have you tear each one of these sermons apart and rewrite it in the light of that motto and that text. I would like to have you so impress your hearers with the glory of your truth that at the end of every service they will feel like grasping each other's hands and eagerly congratulating each other upon the possession of a Gospel more precious than all the gold and jewels in the world.

Prayer to Precede Self-examination

O Gracious Father, grant me such measure of Thy grace that I always may grow in gratitude.

Not with blind eyes and not with deaf ears may I accept the blessings that every day Thou dost shower upon me.

Enable me to seek and to find the best in everything and everybody.

If among Thy children entrusted to my leadership I

detect indifference and evil, help me to deal gently, hope-
fully, tactfully, to the end that I may be truly useful as
a fellow-laborer with Christ.

SEARCHING SELF-EXAMINATION

(These questions are for no eyes but those of the minister himself. Each is to be considered thoughtfully, prayerfully and repeatedly.)

1. Do I sufficiently emphasize to myself the great joy of the Christian life?

   Answer ....

2. Do I think of Jesus as the man of sorrows and forget Him as the man of joy?

   Answer ....

3. Do I ordinarily feel like giving " three cheers for the universe "?

   Answer ....

4. Do I radiate happiness?

   Answer ....

5. Or am I atrabilious?

   Answer ....

6. Do I approach my pulpit with shining face?

   Answer ....

7. Do I appreciate the winning power of a genuine smile?

   Answer ....

8. Do I remember that I must win my parishioners before I can lead them?

   Answer ....

9. Do I speak to my people as I would like to be addressed if I were in a pew?

Answer ....

10. Does my word of criticism arouse assent or indignation?

Answer ....

11. Do I make my suggestions constructive instead of destructive?

Answer ....

12. Have I degenerated from a helpful critic to a chronic fault-finder?

Answer ....

13. Do my people, young or old, regard me as a crank and a kill-joy?

Answer ....

14. Is it barely possible that some of the things that I condemn may not be so dreadful after all?

Answer ....

15. Do I expect by pessimism to develop optimism?

Answer ....

16. Do I think that I can save my people if, by melancholia, I drive them from the church?

Answer ....

17. What great modern preachers have shown the spirit that I ought to develop?

Answer ....

18. Am I familiar with Goldsmith's "Village Preacher"?

Answer ....

19. Do I think persistently enough of the One whom "the common people" heard gladly?

Answer ....

20. Do I send my people away from church with more zest for the Christian life?

Answer ....

After considering all the suggested points, what ought I to do?

What *will* I do?

Prayer: Forgive me, O Father, if I have failed to be glad enough in Thy Gospel or thankful enough for my ministry. Help me to reconsecrate myself to an ever increasing service.

SECTION THREE

MY MIND TO ME A KINGDOM IS

(A teacher offers suggestions for Rev. Elmer M. Bright, other beloved students of former days and any ministers who are disappointed about progress in their profession and are uneasy about their own intellectual habits.)

A MAN trudged bravely through Harvard Yard and rather painfully mounted the steps of Emerson Hall. His locks were gray and his shoulders slightly sagged. A younger minister, recognizing him as one of the country's leading preachers, hastened to overtake him. "Why, Doctor," he said, "I am glad that you are teaching here

at the summer school. What course are you giving?"
"No," replied the eminent man, "I am not giving; I am
taking. I am preparing for the ministry. I do that, you
know, fifty-two weeks each year." He was the same
gifted scholar who rejoiced to quote over and over the
line written three hundred years ago by Edward Dyer,
"My mind to me a kingdom is."

CASE I

A Study Is a Place in Which to Study

Classroom Number 6

Rev. Elmer M. Bright,
Monson, Minn.

My dear Elmer:

You do well, after ten years of pulpit work, to pause for
serious self-examination. A considerable fraction of your
ministry is past—at least a sixth, perhaps a third, possibly even a half. If your homiletic habits are not already
fixed, the probability is that they will be within another
decade; so, if you are ever to make radical improvement
in either method or spirit, "now is the day of salvation."

Inasmuch as you have promised to take no offense, I
shall speak with absolute honesty. You need to have
someone do so. It appears to me that some time ago,
perhaps before your graduation, you came to an intellectual standstill. You were a bright boy then—and now,
at thirty-one, you are still a bright *boy*. Are you willing
to be a chronic juvenile? These sermons would have been
creditable for a sophomore, but they are not even respectable for a man who has had three parishes and who
has had intimate contact with men and women, over-
burdened, pain-wracked, sorrow-broken and sin-dis-
tracted.

You have submitted a sermon on Thanksgiving, the

principal idea of which seems to be that we ought to be grateful that we are better fed than other people, have less sickness and have superior opportunities for culture. Is that really as far as you have thought into the philosophy of thankfulness? You preach about Providence (Jehovah-Jireh) and the religious concepts seem to be those of " The Green Pastures." Here is a discourse on " Sin and Punishment." It is a schoolboy effort, revealing no understanding of modern psychology. The three on " Prayer," " Church Support," and " Stewardship " are no different, as I can see, from some that you might have written in your student days. You seem to have been willing to take your science, philosophy, religion at second hand. Now you are paying the penalty of self-indulgence. Slipshod thinking always results in slipshod minds.

Now, what can you do? At thirty-one you are not too old to turn right about face. When you recover from your surprise and indignation at this letter, you can acknowledge that any subject worth preaching about is worth preaching well about, you can accept your unusual mind as God's command to think clearly, you can repent and consecrate your brain.

First, engrave it on your mental tablets that *a study is a place in which to study*. You will be wise to read the books of men who have given special attention to effective thought. *The Art of Thinking*, by Dimnet, is good and so is *The Art of Learning*, by Pitkin. A classic on the subject is a delightful old book, *The Intellectual Life*, by Philip Gilbert Hamerton.

A busy minister, desiring to be fair to himself, must budget his time and, just as far as possible, must stick to his schedule. He must no more leave out his allotment for mental nourishment than he would that for sleep or physical food.

He must read much and with careful selectivity. Articles and books that repeat his own information and interpretation will demand little time. Those that present new discoveries and fresh theories and especially those that emphasize views different from his own ought to be read with care. He must read conqueringly.

Then there will be works of special value that will need to be not only read but re-read and re-re-read. The distinction between reading and study ought not to be forgotten. Study requires digging. References are carefully followed. Marginal comments are made, or, better still, a notebook is kept, with page by page analysis and argument. No paragraph is dismissed until it is thoroughly understood.

Read much, dear Elmer. Meditate more.

You say that I am advising hard work. Yes. Mental perspiration is as normal as physical perspiration. You are challenged to full mental manhood.

You speak of financial compensation for my counsel. Send nothing. Reward me, if at all, by taking in good spirit my very frank advice and by making your remaining years fine and fruitful. For the Church and the world are in tragic need of ministers such as you might be if you did your best and utmost.

> With deep and abiding affection,
> The Pedagogue Homiletical.

CASE II

The Attraction of Distractions

Dear Oswald:

You pulverize your time. I strongly advise you to reserve each day a certain amount of time, even though it be only a little, when you permit no interruptions for any ordinary cause, but devote yourself assiduously and joyously to the intellectual life. Perhaps this can be at the same time each day; but, in the over-strenuous, hectic life of the present, it probably cannot. Never mind. Save the period *some* time. " Count that day lost whose low descending sun" views from thy mind no careful study done.

Your trouble is that you yield to the attraction of distractions. When you get settled to study, you suddenly remember that you have an important letter to write. Or your garden ought to be weeded. Or the good wife needs a little lift about her housework. Or there is more work to be done on that committee report. Or the tennis court should be used while the sun shines. Or the automobile ought to be washed. And so on and so on.

Those duties and those pleasures all are important and should have a place in your well-balanced life. But they should be absolutely excluded from your thought when you have settled for your hours of concentration.

A certain minister has borrowed from a hotel one of those " Please Don't Disturb " signs that are placed on the doors of somnolescent guests. It is hung on the door of his study when he secludes himself, and maid, wife and children all know that it is to be obeyed. They respect him because they understand that he is performing an important part of " his Father's business."

CASE III

" I Wander and I Wander "

Dear Henry:

You tell me that you find it almost impossible to keep your thoughts concentrated when you are reading or meditating. So you are like the rest of us! That you recognize your difficulty gives hope that you will overcome it.

The undisciplined mind works like this: The printed page brings a reference to the city of Rome; I remember that my friend Rupert was in Italy last summer; I recall that when he started away he was carrying a beautiful new traveling bag; I am pleased that his appreciative parishioners made him such a present; I am reminded that Wife and I must decide upon that wedding present that we must send next week; I wonder what ceremony will be used when Janice and her young man are married; I think that Janice is a beautiful girl, but, somehow, not quite so magnetic as her sister Elizabeth. So I wander and wander until I suddenly glance down at my book and am amazed to see that I have traveled all the way from Rome to little Elizabeth. And I can't think how. Edgar Allan Poe pretended that he could retrace the steps of a wandering mind; but, of course, he could not. No one can.

What can you do about your trouble? Regret it. That will help. Firmly resolve to concentrate. Impress upon yourself the great importance of the matter that you are to read or think about. If you discover that you have erred again, fine yourself, making the penalty serious enough so that your subconscious mind will be impressed. When you succeed in a creditable period of concentration give yourself some reward, also for the benefit of the subconscious. Try, try, try again.

CASE IV

The Wisdom of a Way

Dear Arthur:

Whatever drifts, drifts downstream. A minister ought to have system in his intellectual life as much as a merchant ought to have system in his store or a manufacturer ought to have system in his factory.

You say that you are not getting along as well as you should in what you call your post-college education. Is it because you have not taken time to work out some orderly procedure for your study? You remember, probably, the epigram that good old Doctor Henderson used to repeat so often at theological school: " Plan your work and then work your plan."

I cannot detail what would be the best system for you to follow—inasmuch as every man is a problem by himself and for himself. I can tell you the procedure of one great man who made a success of both his intellectual and his spiritual life.

First he shut himself in his study with locked door and disconnected telephone. He read a passage from the Bible. He made a little prayer. Taking up a book, he decided upon its relative importance. If it were upon some familiar subject, he knew that there was no necessity for him to read it word for word or, perhaps, even paragraph for paragraph. Quickly he could get the author's point of view, sample his literary style, and find in what way his ideas differed from the ideas of others who had written along the same line. He could master that book in a little while, storing in his mental pigeonholes all that was new and important.

Other books, however, required time. There was careful searching to find exact shades of meaning; there was keen criticism of apparent inconsistencies; there was frequent use of pencil and paper, and there was much independent thought in regard to moot points.

Between the volumes that were easy and those that he called " tough " there were some that were comparatively simple or comparatively difficult. He tried to use good sense about them all.

Being a writer as well as a reader, he scorned slipshod work, delighting in the Pauline text, " Study to show thyself approved unto God, a workman that needeth not to be ashamed, rightly dividing the word of truth."

His plan may not be your plan. What I am suggesting, dear Arthur, is that you adopt *some* plan, and persist in it. We read much about "the way of wisdom." Remember also the wisdom of a way.

CASE V

Undigested Securities

Dear Frederic:

In your letter you say, "I read and read and read." Are you quite certain that you therefore are keeping your mind alive and progressive? Do you read and understand and assimilate and classify?

A certain minister spends several mornings a week in a public library, taking pride in being "an omnivorous reader." There is no evidence that he is an omnivorous *student*, which is a very different thing. A friend tells me that he reads every week, in addition to fiction and magazine articles, at least two solid books. Possibly he reads them with profit, for some men can work much more rapidly than others. It is safe to say that not many of us could do so much. I wonder whether he really conquers the difficult paragraphs. I wonder whether he could pass an examination on a scholarly book and get a respectable grade.

A great financier, being asked to explain a current panic, said that it was due to an overabundance of "undigested securities." It is to be suspected that such would be the diagnosis of the mental states of some men who read much rather than well.

I hope, Frederic, that you will have an ideal in your intellectual life. You can go through some books with "a hop, a skip and a leap," for that is all that is necessary for mastery. Others are slow, hard reading. Digest your intellectual securities.

Prayer to Precede Self-examination

O God, in whose service I gladly enlist, keep me aware. Deliver me from all unmindfulness, unmindfulness of Thee, of Thy needy children, of the great privilege of being the messenger of Thy truth and the minister of Thy grace.

In my hours of solitude may I think deeply of Thy parental love and in my hours of utterance may I proclaim with clarity and power Thy glorious Gospel.

So may I earn the privilege of progress.

SEARCHING SELF-EXAMINATION

(These questions are for no eyes but those of the minister himself. Each is to be considered thoughtfully, prayerfully, and repeatedly.)

1. Do I take my thought-life seriously as a sacred responsibility to myself? My family? My church? My country? My God?

   Answer ....

2. Do I remember the Christly commandment to love God with all my *mind?*

   Answer ....

3. Is my culture broader than it was a year ago?

   Answer ....

4. What is my definition of "intellectual respectability"?

   Answer ....

5. Do I meet hard problems with determination or do I dodge and postpone them?

   Answer ....

6. Am I increasing in my power of concentration?

   Answer ....

7. Do I yield too easily to distractions when I ought to be studying?

    Answer ....

8. Am I a day dreamer?

    Answer ....

9. Do I make proper use of libraries?

    Answer ....

10. Do I take advantage of worth-while lectures?

    Answer ....

11. Do I try to keep up with modern scientific information?

    Answer ....

12. Do I try to keep up with modern philosophy?

    Answer ....

13. Do I try to keep up with modern theological thought?

    Answer ....

14. Do I try to keep up with Biblical scholarship?

    Answer ....

15. Do I properly limit the time given to amusements?

    Answer ....

16. Do I allow editors to make up my mind for me?

    Answer ....

17. Do I allow radio commentators to make up my mind for me?

    Answer ....

18. Do I preserve in reading a proper proportion between fiction and more serious works?

    Answer ....

19. Do I sufficiently fear and abhor prejudice?

   Answer ....

20. Do I read principally those authors who express my own beliefs or do I seek stimulation from those who challenge me by disagreement?

   Answer ....

After considering all the suggested points, what ought I to do?

What *will* I do?

Prayer: O God, grant me such measure of Thy grace that, by faithfulness this day, I shall be better fitted for the tasks and problems of tomorrow.

SECTION FOUR

DOWN WITH THOSE BARRIERS!

(The professor feels that some of his former students, including Rev. Clarence Garnerson, are indulging in such pulpit play and display that their usefulness is endangered, and, when they ask his counsel, he speaks to them with unexpected frankness.)

A HUNDRED years ago there was in the United States Senate a man of wide culture but of limited popularity and influence. The trouble with him was that he lacked the good sense to make his superior attainments helpful instead of harmful. He had the appearance of looking down on his less educated colleagues, and no one, in the Senate or out of it, enjoys condescension. On one occasion he introduced in the midst of his speech a long quotation in Latin, although well aware that only a few of his fellows knew what he was saying. Up rose a senator from the frontier and began an address in Choctaw. When the laughter began to subside, the previous speaker remonstrated against the waste of time. " But, Mr. Speaker," said the Westerner, " he can understand me as well as I can understand him, and I submit that I have as much right to address the Senate in Choctaw as he has to bother us with his Latin." There are ministers who turn their culture and their experiences into disadvantages instead of into helps. They seem to set themselves on some higher level than their people. Alas, what a waste! In contrast think of such a man as Dr. Frederick E. Emrich, who could preach fluently in five languages but who never lost the sense of intimate friendship with even the humblest of his hearers.

CASE I

The Preacher from Pisa

Classroom Number 6

Rev. Clarence P. Garnerson,
Essex, New York.

My dear Clarence:

You are turning your advantages into disadvantages. What an extravagance! What a tragedy!

Any acquaintance would say that you have had very unusual advantages and you yourself would be quick to admit it. Let us enumerate. You come from a family of wealth, culture, social position, wide influence. Not many ministers can say that for themselves. You have a comfortable fortune. Almost no minister can say that. You have had a thorough preparation in a college and in a divinity school, both of the highest grade. You have supplemented your American studies with two years of postgraduate work in Europe. You have traveled extensively. You have an ample and well-chosen library. You have abundant memories of the World War. You have a natural disposition to industry and an unusual facility for quick understanding and ready expression. Advantages indeed!

Yet both you and I know that you are not so popular and not so useful as a good many men of your age who have been exceedingly limited in education, experience and resources. You tell me that you are unhappy and I know that you have reason to be. But why are you puzzled?

What you need to understand, Clarence, is that no education is worth much to a minister unless it includes power to keep in close touch and vital sympathy with the people in the pews and that no so-called advantage is helpful to a preacher unless it is used with consummate tact. If a speaker is to influence a congregation month after month he must interest them intellectually and also he must win them personally. Be now warned that if a man is proud of his blessings instead of being humbly grateful for them he is in constant danger of disappointment and failure.

In your own case what should have been avenues of approach have become barriers between you and your people.

I may as well tell you that I knew this before you sent me your batch of sermons. Your settlements have been in the immediate vicinity of our college and I have had frequent opportunities to meet you, to hear you preach and to get confidential reports from your parishioners.

When I have listened to your sermons I have found much to admire; but I have left the churches with a feeling of irritation and antagonism, for I have had a strong impression that you have been " condescending to men of low estate "—of whom I have been one.

I do not wish to be harsh with you, but I think it only fair, now that you have turned to me for counsel, to quote to you some of the remarks that I have heard. " What is the trouble with your church over at Delmarr? " I asked one of your former trustees.

" Oh, the trouble is soon to move to Essex," he replied. Then he said something about " high hat " and " Mr. Toplofty."

One of your present listeners said to me, with a twinkle in his eye, " Mr. Garnerson has had too many trips to Pisa." I didn't catch his meaning at first, so he elaborated.

" He's always telling us," he continued, " about the last time he was in Constantinople, or the last time he went through the Catacombs, or the last time he ascended the Leaning Tower. He gives us the impression that he has the habit of climbing that tower. And, somehow, he loses us common and commonplace people, who never in all our lives have traveled more than a thousand miles. He seems to make himself a being of some superior order."

I have heard much more of the same kind.

Now, here are your six sermons, all revealing clearly why you are not so successful as some of your less favored classmates. It is hardly necessary to say that these sermons are beyond criticism in grammar, rhetoric and homiletics. The trouble with them is that they are *pretentious*. They convey the impression of intellectual pride. They seem to be written by a man who wants to display and emphasize his advanced scholarship and wide travel.

Forgive my bluntness, Clarence, and know that if I thought you were an incurable cad I would not waste time writing this letter.

Here is your sermon on " The Relentless Love," which in many respects is excellent. I will not stop to consider its content; but I call your attention to the fact that you speak of an interpretation that you learned from a great professor during your " postgraduate year at Oxford," of your thrilling experience that you had when your regiment was under fire at Belleau Woods, of a passage that you came across in the library at Berlin, and (can I believe my eyes?) a thought that came to you the last time you climbed the Tower of Pisa. The illustrations all are good, but the reiteration of the capital " I " is not good. Here are your five other sermons, all with possibilities of much usefulness and all practically wasted by an evident pride of self.

You like to quote Greek and Latin. You like to refer often to authors of whom your people presumably never have heard. You like to use polysyllables, even those that you deem it necessary to define. What is your object? The time is long past when ordinary Americans are much impressed by long words and a pretense of profundity.

Dear Clarence, study some of the great preachers of the present. Take Ralph Sockman, whom you and I happen to know quite well. Take McConnell, or Gilroy or Fosdick. These men have traveled far and have learned much. They illustrate freely from all sorts of sources; but, by some subtle good sense, they manage to leave out the offensive personal element. Always they seem to think *with* their hearers, not *down to* them. Remember that distinction.

Yearn for usefulness. Burn with desire to present the truth so that it may make men free. Avoid exhibitionism. Forget yourself. Remember your gospel. Take advantage of your advantages. And go rather seldom to Pisa!

Yours for the goodly fellowship,
The Pedagogue Homiletical.

CASE II

Alter Ego

Dear Bryant:

I never have heard you preach. You open your eyes in amazement and you open your mouth in protest. You remind me that I have been in your congregation dozens of times and that I have shown no signs of either deafness or inattention.

What do I mean? I can make it clear by quoting from a letter recently received:

" We have two ministers," writes Mrs. X. Y. Z. " They have the same name, they live in the same house and they wear the same clothes; but they are two very different men. One we like exceedingly well and the other we—just tolerate. The first one visits in our homes, salutes us on the streets, mingles with us at our socials, consults with us at our business meetings, plays with our children, teaches in our church school. He is a real human. The second preaches to us on Sundays and, oh dear! he is a different somebody, a *very* different somebody. The moment he steps into that pulpit he seems to put on a mask of affectation and artificiality. He seems to move a thousand miles away from us poor mortals to whom he is supposed to deliver the word of life. I do wish, Doctor, that he would ' come to himself.' His real self is very, very good, but this second self is *horrid*."

That letter was not written about you, Bryant, or about anyone of your acquaintance. I don't know, however, that it would have been unjust for one of your members to have written something like that. Your whole personality seems to change when you enter your pulpit. You are no longer the simple, lovable, understandable Bryant Goodwin of the midweek, but you assume an *alter ego*, not so simple, not so lovable and not so understandable. You " put on." And right there you lose your people.

I don't know just why you do it. Perhaps you are the victim of some subconscious imitation of some great orator. Perhaps you are nervous. Perhaps you have an inferiority complex. Whatever the trouble is, conquer it. I shall wander in some Sunday before long and I shall hope to hear *you* preach.

CASE III

Are You an American?

Dear Horace:

I am not an Anglophobe. I am, I trust, an Anglophile. I fear that you are an Anglomaniac.

And by your Anglomania, perhaps unconsciously, you are in danger of transforming your people into Anglophobes—and incidentally of losing your good job.

We had a minister once who tripped over German culture and another who stumbled over Italian art. I suppose there have been those who have fallen over their Americanism.

You, Horace, are in no danger of that third mistake. Here are your six submitted sermons, every one thoroughly English. You quote from English sermons, you refer to English literature, you describe English scenery, you draw illustrations from English life. I have been told, moreover, than you speak with something of an English accent.

Let me see, where were you born? On a farm in New Hampshire! I thought so. How in the world did you get thus expatriated?

Your people are not narrow-minded or chauvinistic. They would welcome rather frequent references to England, France, Russia, Japan and the other great nations.

But they notice your Anglomania and resent it as a pedantic pose. And they would like to see some evidence, once in a while, that you know that there is such a country as the United States of America.

CASE IV

The Outward Man

Dear Spencer:

You resented what I said to you after the occasional sermon at Winstead. You thought that when you asked me for criticism I should have talked about what you said and not about what you wore. Perhaps. Perhaps you are right in saying that your costume is your own business, but you must understand that independence, eccentricity, stubbornness, all may be exceedingly costly.

You prepared an excellent sermon for that convention and then you mounted the platform so dressed that the people discounted your words before you began. Where *did* you get that collar? It must have been in the shop of some theatrical costumer. And where *did* you get that tie? At Harvard? Not even the editors of *The Lampoon* can sport neckwear quite so red.

You demonstrated your American freedom, but the young folks snickered, the old folks shook their heads, and everybody decided that you were a clerical curiosity.

Well, you are not the only man who has lost influence because of costumic whimsicality. You remember the case of our "Duxbury dandy" who so outdressed his parishioners that they thought him vain and in vain. I think that a man serving in the backwoods would be foolish to dress as though he were on Broadway.

We simply have to accept the fact that our people are overcritical about some things that seem insignificant.

One part of ministerial consecration is willingness to yield some little points for the sake of the greater good.

A man's hair is his own and he may think it his privilege to style it according to his own notion. I knew of a clergyman, however, who lost influence because people said that he combed his hair " like a she-girl and not like a he-man."

I am glad, Spencer, that no one ever will have to urge you to personal cleanliness. (Your comic opera collar was spotless!) But some ministers! A preacher not a thousand miles from this school became *persona non grata* because he appeared in church with greasy coat and unpolished shoes. Another gifted man lost a call to a great metropolitan pulpit because he approached the communion table with hands unwashed and nails in mourning.

You are clean in your clothing, dear Spencer. Think over this matter of the outward man and resolve to be clean also in your conscience.

CASE V

Paradise and Perryville

Dear Anthony:

One of your parishioners, touring in Ohio last summer, drove fifty miles out of her way in order to get a glimpse of Perryville. She had heard you speak of it so many times, so many, many times, that she thought that she must see the place at least once before she died. She supposed that it would be, if not so large as New York, at least as extensive as Boston or Philadelphia; she imagined that most of the residences were palatial in size and elegance, and she believed that every estate included a miniature Garden of Eden.

Imagine her surprise when she found that this much-advertised Perryville was, after all, a drab little town, rather less attractive than others that she had visited in the Buckeye State.

You idealize your former home, which is right enough if you are discreet in utterance. Your sermons, however, abound in references to your previous settlement, to the superfine people in the church, to their marvellous ways of transacting business, to the supreme kindness that they showed to their pastor and his wife. A little talk of that kind is likely to be irritating and much of it is sure to become intolerable. Your people are human. After a while some of them will say, " Why did Rev. Anthony Barrows ever leave his heavenly Perryville? " And it will not be long before others will say, " Rev. Anthony Barrows had better return to his *Paradise in Perryville.*"

CASE VI

" Dearly Beloved "

Dear Willard:

You must feel for the hundred and fifty miscellaneous members of your congregation an affection of extreme intensity. At least you tell them so very often in all the sermons that you have sent for my criticism.

Take this first manuscript, the subject of which is, " The Gospel, both Theological and Social." You address your auditors eight times as " Dear friends," five times as " Beloved friends," and five times as " Dearly beloved friends." Well, I am glad that you like your folks!

Really, as you know very well and as your hearers know very well, those phrases mean zero or less than zero. They do not add to your effectiveness, they subtract from it. There was a time when the use of those sentimental forms of address was a homiletical fashion, but now it is a pulpit anachronism. Your parishioners know whether you love them or not, having learned from your daily ministry among them, and they do not need to be reassured at the beginning of every sermonic paragraph.

I sometimes think that even in home life husbands and wives would get along better if they were a little more sparing of their " dears," " darlings," and " sweethearts " and a little more generous in their smiles and kind deeds. At any rate, I am certain that in these days the commonsense men and women in your pews are not won, but are offended, by your perfunctory pet names. Willard, take down that barrier.

PRAYER TO PRECEDE SELF-EXAMINATION

Dear Heavenly Father, by Thy grace help me to accept thoughtfully and thankfully my appointed tasks.

Deliver me from all petty pride and from all that may separate me from my people and lessen the saving power of my message.

Help me to love.

Lift me up in humility.

Make me so irresistibly eager to help those who are entrusted to my care that there may be no barriers between us in thought or in spirit.

SEARCHING SELF-EXAMINATION

(These questions are for no eyes but those of the minister himself. Each is to be considered thoughtfully, prayerfully and repeatedly.)

1. Have I had a feeling that any of the foregoing letters might well have been written to me?

   Answer ....

2. Is my attitude toward my hearers ever one of condescension?

   Answer ....

3. Do I give the apearance of thinking, not with my listeners, but down to them?

   Answer ....

4. Among the names suggested in the concluding paragraph, which would I choose for myself?

   Answer ....

5. Do I refer too often to the travels that I have taken?

   Answer ....

6. Do I quote foreign languages in the pulpit?

   Answer ....

7. Do I make objectionable parade of my Biblical knowledge?

   Answer ....

8. Do I in any way allow my superior culture to separate me from my people?

   Answer ....

9. Do I speak like a heavenly angel addressing a congregation of sinners?

   Answer ....

10. Do I speak like an infallible oracle?

    Answer ....

11. Do I use perfunctorily the phrase, " Dearly beloved," or anything similar?

    Answer ....

12. Do I speak too often of the big city in which I was brought up, of my own fine family or of the wonders of my former parish?

    Answer ....

13. Do I convey the impression that I think some other country is preferable to my own?

Answer ....

14. Do I, when entering the pulpit, assume a different personality?

Answer ....

15. Do I (perhaps unconsciously) imitate some great preacher?

Answer ....

16. Do I overemphasize dignity at the expense of devotion?

Answer ....

17. Do I assume a flippant manner, as though my hearers were second-rate or third-rate people?

Answer ....

18. Do I indulge in offensive oddity in dress?

Answer ....

19. Do I cultivate any other whimsicalities of personal appearance?

Answer ....

20. Am I untidy or uncleanly about my clothing?

Answer ....

After considering all the suggested points, what ought I to do?

What *will* I do?

*Prayer: O God, deliver me from any pride that may go
before a fall. O God, keep me fervid in my
apostleship and grant me progress in helpfulness.*

Section Five

"IT FITS"

(The friendly teacher, reading some sermons of Rev. C.
Clement Willison and other former students, offers some
helpful advice in regard to the congruities of homiletic
work.)

Russell H. Conwell counselled a group of young
clergymen to endeavor not to say the wrong thing, not to
say the right thing in the wrong way, and not to say the
right thing in the right way at the wrong time. It was
proper for him to give that sage advice, for he always
exemplified good sense and good taste.

This man, who, from his fees for his lecture on *Acres
of Diamonds,* made possible the education of hundreds
of young men and women, was as many-sided as any
speaker before the American public. He was a natural
comedian and could convulse any audience with laughter.
He had the power also to reduce them to tears by his
pathos or to lift them to spiritual fervor by his intense
religious oratory. With his many gifts, however, he never
forgot his whenness and whereness.

Some people who had heard him lecture and had
"laughed until their sides ached" went to hear him
preach, with the expectation that they would have other
royal jokes. They never got them. They heard excellent
sermons, happy in spirit and tellingly illustrated, but they
never heard anything that was cheap or out of place or
that might better have been left unsaid. He was all

things to all men—always with a perfect sense of the appropriate.

CASE I

Everything in Its Place

Classroom Number 6

Rev. C. Clement Willison,
Pine Plains, Pennsylvania.

My dear Clement:

The other day Professor Garrett's little Phyllis, aged nine, came over to make a formal call on the lady of my heart, aged fifty-nine. She is a radiant damsel, and, as might be expected if heredity counts for anything, full of original thoughts and expressions. Striving to describe a young woman whom she greatly admires, she exclaimed, " Well, the sum and substance of it all is that she *just belongs.*"

If you knew the object of her enthusiasm you would at once admit the accuracy of the description. When Phyllis gets older she may use the expression, " a harmonious ensemble," in giving a picture of her friend Julia. I myself have been charmed by the excellent taste displayed by this very attractive young American. It matters not what the occasion may be, she always hits upon the exactly appropriate costume. The color is right for her personality. The simple jewelry is not too conspicuous. Her hair is properly arranged. As Phyllis said in attempting to elaborate her description, " Julia *fits.*"

How fortunate indeed is any man or woman who has developed a reliable instinct for the eternal fitness of things! Do you remember Elsie Doremus, who used to live on University Avenue? She is an artist now and I have great hopes for her, because every one of her pictures " just belongs." She seems to have an unerring perception of proportion and propriety. There is an estate up in Lenox that you and I used to admire together. What is its charm? To use another expression borrowed from young Phyllis, " it matches itself." The house, an architectural masterpiece, is in exact keeping with the grounds, the backgrounds, the shrubbery, and the other buildings. There is much variety but there is " unity in variety." I think that one of the supreme charms of Beethoven is that in his music every bar is in essential keeping with the entire composition.

Happy, thrice happy, is the preacher who possesses a quick and accurate judgment as to exactly what is appropriate for homiletical use and exactly what is suitable for any particular sermon. A lady yesterday paid this tribute to her pastor, a man whom both you and I know and love, " I never have to worry about Dr. Greenhalge, but I can always be comfortably assured that I need not be ashamed to have my best friends listen to his sermons." That does not mean that she is in agreement with some of his very radical theories, theological and economic, or that she expects him to be silent regarding what he thinks to be true and right. She, however, trusts his taste.

Now, Clement, you must not be offended if I say that you seem to be more than a little lacking at this point. I have read and reread all of the sermons that you mailed to me. I have found much to admire in them all (especially in the one entitled, " The Paradox of Christianity "), but I am compelled to say that in some details your sermons do not seem to " belong." There are strange incongruities, astonishing lapses from good judgment. I think that your hearers would feel vaguely uneasy about some of them and that they would feel disturbed and shocked about others. They would be likely to remember, moreover, just the unfortunate points.

The uneasiness that I mention is likely to result when you fail to adopt a homilectical method in keeping with your general theme. Some sermons are poetic in thought and others are prosaic. Each should be developed accordingly. Here is one entitled, " The Wings of the Morning." I congratulate you on its many obvious excellencies. I cannot commend you, however, for constructing what is essentially a poem upon the identical plan that you would use for a carefully argued thesis. Look at that outline: four divisions, each with subdivisions, some with sub-subdivisions, all stated as a lawyer might present points in his brief.

In your sermon on " The Christian and War," which is argumentative in its general character, you have used the same homiletic scheme and the effect has been powerful. In that war sermon, however, there is something else that might make the listener wonder just what was out of harmony. In this case it is your incongruous language. You are conducting an argument but you are using the language of poetry. To win in debate you must use simple words, probably short ones, with few figures of speech. You must establish your points in a straightforward way, so that " all twelve men on your jury " can understand and remember them. Profuse ornamentation is not only unnecessary but probably fatal. The other day I read a sermon by another writer that reminded me of a woman who would go to her business office in a dinner gown. It simply didn't " match itself."

I said that I found in your discourses other features that would disturb or offend your judicious auditors. Some of your expressions are quite out of place in the pulpit, being cheap, vulgar, sensational. Far be it from me to suggest that a church ought to be a place of gloom or exaggerated dignity. It should be, of course, a place of good cheer. I think that there is no objection to occasional hearty humor, if it comes naturally and is not lugged in for its own sake. A minister should remember, however, where he is standing, whose apostle he is, and to what sadly needy men and women he is proclaiming the gospel. Do you feel quite comfortable when in the pulpit you tell a funny story that might be entirely appropriate before a Rotary Club? I suspect that you try to make a sensation with what you may call "wise-cracks," but where you have put them they are anything but wise.

Some of your illustrations seem in dreadfully poor taste. "*Tempus fugit* but women fidget." "Adam and Eve were snaked out of Eden." "St. Paul was a bachelor and had to sew on his own buttons." The superficial may giggle but better judges inwardly groan. You have frequent jokes or supposed jokes at the expense of Mrs. Willison and others aimed at the spinsters of your community. *Please* don't.

I am sorry to have you use that parody of the Twenty-third Psalm. Parodies are poor fun in almost any case, but this one on a passage of supreme beauty and very sacred associations is the worst I ever have seen. If you want to indulge in stale humor about a well-known automobile do it somewhere else, but if you really must do it in the pulpit find some other medium for your frivolity than a paraphrase of the Shepherd Psalm.

Dear Clement, I trust you to understand that, even if I speak strongly and even severely, I do it with the kindest of motives. You have so much ability and so much nobility that you are worth saving for the ministry. Give up your ambition to be a comedian in the pulpit. Match your good intentions with good sense. Criticize your own efforts more searchingly than anyone else would do. Make certain that every part of every sermon "belongs."

Yours for power in the Gospel,

The Pedagogue Homiletical.

CASE II

"*You Ain't Him*"

Dear Bertram:

An old farmer years ago gave to a young theologue

some wise and much needed advice. It hurt but it helped. He said, "You ain't him." The budding preacher had been reading the sermons of Lyman Abbott, then at the zenith of his power and influence, and he had been enthralled. So he tried to adopt the literary style of a man who had been preaching forty years and who, in the beginning, had a personality utterly different from his own. The imitation was ridiculous and disastrous. His countryman friend knew the Abbott sermons and was keen enough to recognize the young man's folly. "Be yourself, young feller," he said; "be yourself and be yourself just as good as you can."

That advice, frankly given by the rural sage, was worth a whole term in theological school. If it could be given with convincing power to every divinity student we would have a stronger Christian Church.

God gives to every man a distinct personality. It should be received with gratitude and developed to its fullest potency. By imitation of someone else that personality is weakened or sacrificed.

What would the farmer say to you if he were alive and could read these manuscripts that you have sent? I am afraid that he would shake his head at your super-hyperboles, your dizzy flights of oratory, your overdrawn illustrations. And he might say, "Young feller, you ain't Billy Sunday."

CASE III

A Dozen Blue Pencils

Dear Luther:

You can buy blue pencils at fifty cents a dozen. Blessed little partners they are, indispensable in the editor's sanctum and of great potential usefulness in the minister's study. Luther, you had better invest a half a dollar.

Your submitted sermons are on important subjects, they are well constructed, and, for the most part, they contain excellent English. There are passages, however, that make me cringe and shiver. There are some that might cause sensitive hearers to absent themselves from your future services.

I refer to your frequent lapses from exalted expression into commonplace idiom and current slang. Such departures are not wicked, but they are not wise. What do you think you gain when, in the midst of noble exhortation, you suddenly tell the fathers and mothers in Israel that it is time for them to " hump themselves for the Kingdom "? Or why do you say that the Bishops had better " sit up and take notice "? Or of what advantage is it to say that Saint Paul regarded young Timothy as " a humdinger "? I suppose you think that you can wake up the semisomnolent parishioners by these descents from dignity, but I warn you that you lose more than you gain. Even people who themselves use slang in every sentence shrink from its incongruity in the pulpit.

Do you know the famous anagram, " O, Lor', shop language rises "? Transpose these letters and you will find, " Our slang phraseologies." Shop language may be all right in shops but it is out of place in Christian pulpits.

So use your blue pencils on your slang, and use them with double vigor on your profanity. I deplore the growing custom among our younger ministers (and some of our older ministers) of using language in the pulpit that would shock their hearers on the street. You say, " For God's sake " and, " In God's name," thus trying to show your intensity in exhortation. Scratch out all such expensive expletives.

Moreover, I notice two or three stories, pat to be sure and not absolutely coarse, but more appropriate for a Rotary Club than for a Christian church. You had better scratch them out.

Study the congruities.

CASE IV

A Little Church Around a Corner

Dear Marvin:

The Bishop preaching in his cathedral uses several phrases indicating the dignity and impressiveness of the building in which he is privileged to officiate. He speaks of " this house of beauty," " this holy temple," " this altar of the Most High," " this stately sanctuary," " this noble structure." Well and good.

Astonishingly, I find the same phrases in your sermons, phrases that you apply to your own little chapel. Your building is a tiny, modest structure, adequate for the little band of earnest Christians that you have gathered, but it requires a strong imagination to think of it as a temple, a stately sanctuary, or even a house of beauty. And what about an " altar "? I do not remember that you had one when I visited you last October.

You had better avoid those hifalutin names that bring smiles to the faces of the discriminating listeners.

CASE V

Before the Broken Bread

Dear Ferdinand:

You have included in your batch of sermons two that were designed for pre-Communion delivery. Do you think that you hit the mark with them? One is historical and one is argumentative. It is proper for you to acquaint your people with the history of the Holy Supper and it is your privilege to convince them, if you can, that the particular theory of the Eucharist held in our church is correct. I wish, however, that you would find some other occasion than the hour just preceding the deeply spiritual ceremony. What you need to do on Communion Sunday is to bring your people into the *mood* for fellowship with their brethren, their Christ and their God. That mood is not primarily intellectual. It is in the best sense emotional. Think of that before your next Communion day and preach a sermon that will open the hearts of the hearers to the influences that are divinest and most ennobling.

PRAYER TO PRECEDE SELF-EXAMINATION

O Thou who dost honor me with a call to Thy service, help me to develop an instinct for propriety and proportion.

In my ministry may I do everything decently and in order. Help me always to remember the fitness of things, places and people.

SEARCHING SELF-EXAMINATION

(These questions are for no eyes but those of the minister himself. Each is to be considered thoughtfully, prayerfully and repeatedly.)

1. Have I developed a sense of the fitness of things?

   Answer ....

2. Am I quick to detect incongruities in the work of others?

   Answer ....

3. Am I quick to detect and remedy threatened incongruities in my own work?

   Answer ....

4. Do I properly adjust my sermons to the times in which I speak?

Answer ....

5. Do I properly adjust my sermons to the particular occasions on which I speak?

Answer ....

6. Do I remember sufficiently the recent experiences of those who are to listen?

Answer ....

7. Do I make my sermons seasonable?

Answer ....

8. Is my language too poetic for my theme?

Answer ....

9. Is my language too prosaic for my theme?

Answer ....

10. Do I refer to my modest church building as a temple or cathedral?

Answer ....

11. Do I use slang in the pulpit?

Answer ....

12. Do I indulge in expressions that are offensively extravagant?

Answer ....

13. Do I use words that are indelicate for mixed congregations?

Answer ....

14. Do I introduce wise-cracks that may not be wise?

Answer ....

15. Do I make undue use of pathos?

Answer ....

16. Do I use parodies of sacred selections?

    Answer ....

17. Do I (perhaps unconsciously) use material that would be appropriate for a great orator but is out of place for me?

    Answer ....

18. Do I (perhaps unconsciously) use material that would be appropriate for a traveling evangelist but is out of place for me?

    Answer ....

19. Did my sermon last Sunday morning " match itself "?

    Answer ....

20. Will the sermon that I am preparing for next Sunday " match itself "?

    Answer ....

After considering all the suggested points, what ought I to do?

What *will* I do?

Prayer: Follow me with Thy grace, dear Father God, that with singleness of heart I may speak Thy word and do Thy work.

SECTION SIX

" EVERYTHING CONSIDERED "

(To an interesting group of counsel-seeking young ministers, of whom Rev. Manley Faraday is one, the professor suggests very careful thought in making each sermon fit the locality, the time, the place, the personnel of the audience.)

THE competent surgeon tries to get all possible information about his patient, knowing the importance of " the personal equation." The gifted teacher understands that each pupil is a problem by himself and appropriately adapts his matter and his method. So Phillips Brooks said that he never prepared a sermon without remembering " all the differentials "—personal, local, chronological, circumstantial. Who? Where? When? Why? Thus every utterance became a *special* discourse. Such is common sense. Is it also common practice? It is possible that a preacher may sit down in his study and work out " just another sermon." If he does he must not be surprised if he fails to interest and influence anybody in particular.

CASE I

Who Lives at Canaan Corners?

Class Room Number 6

Rev. Manley Faraday,
Canaan Corners, Texas.

My dear Manley:
  You have forgotten something. You have forgotten something exceedingly important.
  It is in my heart to speak to you gently and also grate-

fully, for your six submitted sermons show that you have been reading widely and thoughtfully and that you have not refused to do persistent, arduous work. I say to you frankly that I would be proud to hear you deliver any of these sermons in a college chapel and I think several of them worthy of publication in a religious journal.

Nevertheless, you are in trouble. Your congregations are small and are getting smaller and smaller. Your leading people are inattentive and unresponsive. Sometimes your deacons fall asleep during the passages upon which you have burned most midnight electricity. You have a sense of futility and are aware that your resignation would not be unwelcome.

And I do not wonder. You have forgotten *who lives at Canaan Corners*. I strongly suspect that every week you prepare sermons, not for John Robinson, " general merchant," or for Chloe Sherman, relict of old Captain Sherman, or for Mr. and Mrs. Jasper Clark, indigent hero and heroine of an ancient and exhausted farm, but for the absent president of your college, the dean of your theological school, or the erudite wife of Senator Gladdings.

Your very titles betray you: " Esoteric Christianity," " The Coming Theodicy," " Ideals and the Ultimate," " Evolution and Teleology," " The Search for the Absolute," " The God-Intoxicated Spinoza." Four of the six sermons begin with scholarly expositions of involved and difficult texts, interesting enough for some people, but likely to send Jared Smithkins wool-gathering before you even get under way.

Consider the following paragraph from a recent number of *The Writer:*

" There is a type of manuscript which comes to the editor with dismaying frequency, the article which is good so far as its subject is concerned but is rejected because its writer has failed to visualize the typical reader of the publication to which he submits it. He makes use of a vocabulary which is away over the reader's head or of technical expressions which the reader cannot understand."

There are preachers who are as guilty of psychological ineptitude as that would-be author.

Have you ever attended many sessions of court? That is one way in which a minister can get valuable education. If you go some time you will be likely to hear some blundering lawyer delivering a learned argument to the judge, who needs no guidance, instead of to the jury, whom he is supposed to convert. Manley, you have been making a similar mistake.

Just who are the people at Canaan Corners? Good, wholesome, common-sense, middle-class Americans, ordinary folks with ordinary burdens, griefs, pains, temptations, disappointments, problems. How many of them have been to college? Not one. To normal school? Perhaps two or three. Yet you talk to them as though they had taken postgraduate work at Harvard or at Oxford.

I am not saying that you have uneducated or unintelligent parishioners. Probably some of them can perform skillfully a hundred tasks about which a college professor would blunder or fail altogether. They perhaps could overwhelm him at checkers or chess. It may be that they are more sensible than he at the ballot box. They have culture, but it is a different culture from that of the class room or the study.

You are not to worry about preaching " over the heads of your people." Some cautious ministers are troubled on that point, when the fact is that they are preaching to *other* heads. The lack is with them, not with their parishioners. They need to learn how to find " the point of contact " and then keep it. It is said that the teachings of Jesus were so profound that even the simplest folks could understand them. The most skillful preacher the world ever has known spoke to common people about common things—fish, wheat and tares, wayside flowers, mustard seed, shepherds—and to unlettered peasants he conveyed the highest truth that ever entered human minds.

Reading through your sermons I find that they presuppose, on the part of your listeners, study that they surely have had no opportunity to give. Here in one place you refer to " the Mendelian law." Your trustees would wonder whether that referred to some statute of the ancient Romans or to a Swedish plan for controlling the liquor traffic. Here you speak of " a bygone anthropomorphism." Here you mention " the quantum theory." Here you draw an illustration from " the Pre-Raphaelites." Oh, Manley!

Not only is such " fine writing " unintelligible to the average churchgoer, it is positively offensive. It gives the auditor the impression that the preacher is trying to show off. The conviction that the minister is consumed with intellectual pride, whether true or not, alienates the listeners and makes them immune to his best intended service.

Dear fellow, with your rare possibilities, you surely must adjust yourself to usefulness. I want you to burn with eagerness to help your sadly puzzled people. When you commence to prepare a sermon, bring before your mind's eye the collection of God's common people who are likely to be in your pews. What can you do for Mrs. Farnum, who is perplexed about her wandering boy? For Mr. Jacobs, who has many debts but few dollars? For Miss Golding, who has been told by her specialist, " not more than six months at most "? For poor Jim Matthews, who is deathly sick of his besetting sin? For Widow Mallory, who every night is too tired to rest? For little Sally Blaine, who at eighteen is the only survivor of seven children?

I submit that none of these hungry hearers will be greatly helped by your quotation from Herbert Spencer:

" Evolution is an integration of matter and a concomitant dissipation of motion, during which the matter passes from an indefinite homogeneity to a definite, coherent heterogeneity, and during which the retained motion undergoes a parallel transformation."

Yours with unbounded good will,

The Pedagogue Homiletical.

CASE II

Heterogeneous Hamilton

Dear Leon:

You may as well face the fact that, like most ministers, you have a mixed congregation. Keep your situation constantly in mind when you prepare your sermons.

Behold, how different is your problem from that of a visiting lecturer! The minister must try to reach a heterogeneous congregation while the lecturer has the advantage of a homogeneous audience. At the University the other night we had the joy of listening to Dr. Sterling, world-famous astronomer. Every person there was interested in astronomy and astronomers—else he would not have paid a good round price for a ticket of admission. Every person there was from the college group and had a considerable degree of culture. All were receptive and responsive.

But at the Hamilton church on Sunday morning! Poor Leon! You are expected to reach and inspire and save many men of many minds—and some of exceedingly little minds. What a strange mixture of humanity you have in your constituency! Master and maid! Grandfather and grandchild! Saint and sinner! Optimist and pessimist! And from what a variety of experiences do they assemble for the hour of supposed worship! One is elated with success and one is cast down with awful failure. One is glowing with health and one is racked with physical agony. One is sound in Christian faith and one is heretical in both morals and religion.

You write that your sermons do not seem to " click." Can it be because you have not stopped to consider carefully this extreme difficulty that confronts you and nearly every other minister? Perhaps you preach to the most cultured faction, perhaps to the least cultured, perhaps to the old, perhaps to the young, perhaps to the rich, perhaps to the poor. There is even a possibility that you preach at random.

You are kind enough to ask my counsel, and, just as formerly at the university, I reply in the spirit of an elder brother.

I think that, like the rest of us, you need to find the common denominator.

Discard at once the thought that you must instruct your highly educated parishioners on matters about which they probably know far more than you do. They do not attend church to acquire further information in regard to science, literature or philosophy. They yearn to escape for a little while from the routine of their work and to get a vision of something else. They hunger for vital religion and they seek for the truth that maketh free. Can you give them something that will comfort them in their sorrow and inspire them in their dejection? Neither offend them with vulgarity and inanity nor bore them with classroom surpluses.

The fact is, the central facts of the Christian gospel are both simple and sublime. God, unfailing in love and wisdom; Christ, suffering gladly for humanity's sake; sin, hindering the Infinite good will; brotherhood, the normal relationship for individuals and for nations; hope, founded in the character of the sufficient Deity—such are the great fundamentals of your beautiful message. They are needed by the high and the low. Your task is to illustrate and enforce these truths in such a way that both the illiterate and the learned, both the evil and the good, both the favored and the unfortunate, will accept them and be touched and ennobled.

This may not be as difficult as you think. Your simple folks may understand much more than you suppose, and your cultured folks may be more responsive to plain speaking on plain topics.

Paul solved this problem. Great modern preachers have solved it. Thousands of faithful ministers, making no pretensions to greatness, have solved it. Taking due thought, you can solve it.

CASE III

Fact—Plus

Dear Ralph:

You are an enthusiast for fact. Good. Now try to be an enthusiast for tact. Some ministers are strong on fact, but weak on tact. Their pastorates are brief. Others are strong on tact but weak on fact. Their pastorates are futile.

You write, somewhat complainingly, that you have a parish full of peculiar people. Well, then, adjust yourself to their idiosyncrasies.

There was a great Christian preacher whose name was Paul, and he testified of himself, " I am made all things to all men that I might by all means save some." He meant, of course, all things true and honorable and worthy of his apostleship.

I think from what I hear from you and from what I hear about you that you lack something of his consecrated adaptability. You behold something wrong in your church or your community and you make your attack with utter courage but with little wisdom. You do not stop to consider place or occasion. It seems to be your motto to " hit them often and to hit them hard."

You "hew to the line and let the chips fall where they will."

You will gain no friends in that way and you will never reform the world in that way. You will simply lose your influence and your positions.

You will ask if you ought not to speak the truth. Yes, but in proper place and in proper spirit. Possibly, if you have a parishioner who is guilty of some great indiscretion the proper place may be in the privacy of his own home rather than in the publicity of your pulpit.

I notice that in your sermons you take little disagreeable flings at the whims, prejudices and foibles of your people. What do you expect thus to accomplish? Anything except to alienate those who ought to be your supporters and those whom, by wiser methods, you might direct to better ways?

Just as there are sins of commission and sins of omission, there are also virtues of commission and virtues of omission. I wish that you had omitted a good many harmful statements from your sermons—though they may be perfectly true.

Study what to omit, what to postpone, what to say privately. And study to speak with good will, good grace, and good sense.

When I was married, lo these many years ago, a wise friend commended to me the twin angels "Bear and Forbear." I commend and recommend them to you and to every minister of Christ.

CASE IV

"Days Like These"

Dear Orrin:

This morning's mail brings two batches of sermons, one from you and one from one of your respected classmates. Glancing through them, I am favorably impressed with them all. I perceive, however, one very great difference.

All twelve of these discourses have been prepared during a period of national and international contention and crisis. Your friend preaches every week about the particular problems of the present war. On the other hand, you seem entirely and astonishingly oblivious of any conditions out of the ordinary.

Would it not be wise for both of you to strike a happy medium? As you know, I sit in a pew more than half the Sundays in a year and therefore I know something about the layman's point of view. We listeners would be in danger of nervous and spiritual prostration if Doctor Halliman devoted the whole of every sermon, week after week, to the horrors of contemporary life and the pressing problems that confront our country. Newspapers and magazines are full of hard problems and agonizing reports. We go to church for something else.

The dear Doctor would seem strange, however, if he totally ignored the unique circumstances of the day. He shows admirable good sense and tact, presenting the eternal gospel with charm and power, and emphasizing the fact that it ought to be applied in all the great exigencies of life. He preaches no escapism. He encourages no foolish serenity. He makes occasional very telling references to the present world conditions. He does not overdo.

You and your fellow student ought to hear Doctor Halliman and take note of his excellent judgment. Every week he sends us home, fortified in spirit and more eager to be respectable citizens of our country and of the world.

CASE V

Something for Each

Dear Sidney:

One of your intelligent parishioners made a significant

remark about your successful pulpit work. She said,
" He always says at least one thing that seems especially
for me, something that I can take home and remember."
So she congratulated herself that in a year she had at
least fifty helpful suggestions to write in her notebook
and to engrave for permanent preservation on her mental
tablets.

Hearing you preach and reading some of your sermons,
I believe that you do for others what you do for her. You
are blessed with the knack of making your thought vivid
and emphatic to different people, so that each will receive
something of permanent value. Happy Sidney! I wish
that we all were as gifted and as wise.

I have used you as an illustration in urging this matter
upon our present students.

I have told them, also, about the beloved Doctor Bran-
don, who was our pastor during my childhood and youth.
Every Sunday he hit each member of our family. Mother
thought the sermon was for her, Father was convinced
that it was for him, and I *knew* it was for me. I have no
doubt that in his preparation he thought of differing
groups and designed something especial for each.
Sometimes, no doubt, he thought of individuals. I still
remember illustrations that he threw in particularly for
the children.

In your parish you have an unusual situation. The
orphanage group, compelled to be in the pews, might get
restless and troublesome, if you were not so thoughtful
and tactful. The lawyers, in your church because you
are settled at the county seat, are tired and might get
sleepy. The young parents need to be told that there is
something in their lives more important than the levities
of the Couple's Club. The traveling men who come in
from the hotel are mind-hungry and soul-hungry. The
widows, of whom you have your share, deserve to be
comforted and encouraged. For all these and others you
do well to present a specialized gospel.

Keep it up. Don't slip into generalities. Generalities generally do not generate.

PRAYER TO PRECEDE SELF-EXAMINATION

Almighty and all-loving God, I thank Thee that Thou hast called me to sacred fellowship and apostleship.

Grant unto me a passion for helpfulness.

Deliver me from all false pride and vainglory.

Give me mighty enthusiasm for mankind and a tender sympathy for all Thy struggling children.

Whenever I rise to speak forth Thy truth, may it be with no selfish and senseless ambition but with a heart single for the cure of souls.

SEARCHING SELF-EXAMINATION

(These questions are for no eyes but those of the minister himself. Each is to be considered thoughtfully, prayerfully and repeatedly.)

1. Are there any points in this section that suggest short-comings of my own?

   Answer ....

2. Do I forget just what people compose my congregation?

   Answer ....

3. Do I preach as though all my hearers wore Phi Beta Kappa keys?

   Answer ....

4. Am I given to pompous expression?

   Answer ....

5. Do I use a magazine style instead of a pulpit style?

   Answer ....

6. Do I allow technical terms to becloud my utterances?

Answer ....

7. Are my illustrations such as strike home with the particular people who listen?

   Answer ....

8. Am I too much influenced by the literary style of eminent preachers?

   Answer ....

9. Am I trying to imitate somebody or just to be my own best and strongest self?

   Answer ....

10. Am I eager, first of all and most of all, to reach my hearers with comfort, inspiration and guidance?

    Answer ....

11. Do I confuse oratory with apostleship?

    Answer ....

12. Do I sufficiently consider and frankly accept the fact of the heterogeneity of my audience?

    Answer ....

13. Am I determined that not a single listener shall go away from a service without having received some helpful and rememberable truth?

    Answer ....

14. Am I careful to make my sermons simple enough for my ordinary parishioners and yet intellectually respectable for the more cultured?

    Answer ....

15. Do I properly provide for the younger members of my congregation?

Answer ....

16. Am I careful to make my preaching up to date?

Answer ....

17. Do I preach exclusively or too much about the world conditions of this present time?

Answer ....

18. Do I let my courage run away with my good judgment?

Answer ....

19. Do I let my tact run away with my courage?

Answer ....

20. Do I remember that the least agreeable and responsive people in the congregations are the ones who most need the Christian message?

Answer ....

After considering all the suggested points, what ought I to do?

What *will* I do?

Prayer: Accept me, O God, as Thy partner in the Gospel, and help me to make every utterance magnetic and efficient.

BY WAY OF ILLUSTRATION

(The teacher, deeply interested in the usefulness of his former pupils, considers the sermons of Rev. Philo Warmington and some of his colleagues, and is moved to offer counsel in regard to an important matter of homiletical technique.)

A PARISHIONER of Henry Ward Beecher said, "My minister makes his sermons *shine*." Beecher has been called the greatest modern master of illustration. To read his published works is to understand why that tribute has been given. Such variety! Such vividness! Such vigor! If it is delightful to read them, what must it have been to have heard them delivered by that man of flashing eye and obedient voice! What was his secret? His power came from his purpose. He wanted to impress the supreme truth of which he believed himself the custodian and apostle. That was what made him eager in his search for exactly the simile, the quotation, the story, that would make his thought clear and permanent in the minds of his listeners. There was no exhibitionism. There was determination to present his truth so that to even the duller members of his congregation it might be understandable, magnetic and transforming.

CASE I

Just Enough of a Good Thing

Classroom Number 6

Rev. Philo Warmington,
Plainville, Florida.

My dear Philo:

Your submitted sermons are timely in topic, noble in spirit, and, so far as I can judge, sound in doctrine.

In one matter, that of illustration, they are in radical contrast with some that I received the other day from a former student not of your acquaintance. That dear fellow had worked hard and had produced a series of discourses that had much merit; but in the whole batch, enough to fill a third of a volume, there was not a single metaphor, simile, quotation, literary allusion, anecdote or instance from life. For the preacher—the acme of weariness! For the hearers—the climax of dreariness! Every minister needs to know that no ordinary congregation can swallow its homiletical potions without a fair proportion of palatable illustrations.

Now, Philo, you never will be accused of being niggardly with your illustrative material. You go to the other extreme with a vengeance! Once, in preaching class, a student brought in a sermon that so superabounded in illustrations that both pupils and faculty were nearly frantic, and when, at the period of criticism, he was told that he had too many stories, he said, " Oh, but, Professor, I knew them all and I thought that I must put them all in! " I now remind you that that young man was named Warmington. Do you recall that because you cut out such an amazing number of quotations and stories the fellows nicknamed you " the Yankee Clipper "?

Let us look at one of your sermons. Here is one on " Walking with the Master," founded on Gladden's beautiful hymn and introducing many noble and uplifting thoughts. It begins with an interesting reference to a celebrated symbolical painting. It contains quotations, mostly brief, from Emerson, Carlyle, Parker, Channing, an unnamed historian, a friend in Connecticut, Howells, Jerome, Tertullian, a Scotch clergyman, Paul, Confucius, a Roman priest, someone, Descartes, Bryant, a clergyman, another, Gladden, Tennyson, Beecher. It has nine passages from the Gospels, two poems of sixteen lines each, five fragments of verse, five " human interest stories," four accounts of *Walks with the Master* taken by Father Damien, Dr. Grenfell, Jane Addams, and Albert Schweitzer. All this in a sermon that would be delivered in about half an hour! Moreover, there is a cloud of figurative language from beginning to end.

This sermon on " Discipleship for Today " is open to similar comment. So, indeed, are these on " The Country of Which Washington was the Father," " A Religious Technocrat," " The Soul's Housecleaning," and " Missions Nevertheless." You need, tragically, the sense of proportion.

Consider that always your illustration is for the sake of your truth, not vice versa. Over illustration is quickly tiresome, it gives the sense of superficiality, it leads to the suspicion that you are laboring to be poetic or eloquent or that you are substituting ornament for further material. Too many raisins spoil your pudding. Too many pictures spoil your wall.

More serious to the friendly critic than the multiplicity of your illustrations is their apparent lack of spontaneity. In spite of their great number, I get the impression that they do not spring happily from your own mind as a part of your vigorous thought about your theme, but are tacked on, as though you felt yourself in duty bound to use them. Where do you get them? From some of those H-H-H-H books for ministers (Handy Homiletic Hints and Helps)? I suspect it from the fact that you are using stories that were worn out when my grandfather was an infant. Consider your venerable tale (of doubtful authenticity) about the crew, dying from thirst, that finally obeyed the signal, " Let down your buckets where you are," and found that it was sailing through fresh water at the mouth of the Amazon. That story may have had power a century ago, but it deserves a long rest in the museum of homiletical antiquities.

Try in all cases to have your illustration vital in your own mind and not merely adopted from some other speaker. That does not mean that you are never to use what someone else has used. Of course, some figures, sentiments, anecdotes, are quoted and requoted time and time again. What I do mean is that you should use no illustration until you have thoroughly assimilated it and made it part of your own mental reservoir.

Read the sermons of Spurgeon, Brooks, Newton, Mc-Connell, Hough, Cadman, and other masters of illustration. Read, not to borrow or imitate, but to observe how fresh and pat and intimate every illustration is. No books of stock material for them!

Newton quotes much from ancient and modern literature, each passage being one that has impressed him in his omnivorous reading and become a part of himself. No doubt he has some personal plan of marginal marking. Possibly he assists his memory by a system of filing. But he uses nothing that is not intellectually his own.

Fosdick scintillates with all sorts of illustrations, secured from all sorts of places; but all are digested, assimilated, made part of himself. When, for instance, he quotes Mencken as calling man " a local disease of the cosmos—a kind of pestiferous eczema," or when he quotes Martineau as declaring, " What we can say about God to what is left unsaid is as the raindrop to the firmament," he is not drawing from any preachers' handbook, he is recalling something that in his own reading struck him with tremendous force and made a permanent impression.

Read daily with the thought that you are to meet illustrations for your sermons. Read your newspaper with your pencil in hand and your notebook ready. Has the custom house excluded the reproduction of Michael Angelo's paintings? Has a scientist admitted that, after all, the universe may have a spiritual interpretation? Has Patri given wise advice about adolescent boys? Has a man deserted his family on the ground that he must " live his own life "? Has an editor written a worth-while leader on taxation? It's all grist for your mill. In like spirit, keep alert when you read magazines and books and when you listen to lectures or important conversation. And, after all, your own meditations ought to yield your best illustrations.

Send me some more sermons, Friend Philo. Use about one-fourth as many illustrations. Have every one vitally your own.

Yours for hard work and good work,

The Pedagogue Homiletical.

CASE II

I Don't Believe You

Dear Bertrand:

Let me see, just how old are you? Not even one score years and ten! By the number of tales you tell in your sermons and by their variety and strangeness I would think that you must be at least an octogenarian.

You make me think of a traveling preacher I once heard who related so many episodes in his life that the incredulous in his congregation calculated that he must be over a hundred and fifty years of age.

Why do you do it? I don't believe you, partly because I know that some of the stories of which you make yourself the hero are taken from well-known books of illustrations. Whether they ever were true about anybody I don't know, but I am certain they are not true about scores of unwise ministers who tell them in the first person.

Did you really see that lunar rainbow that you so vividly describe? Lunar rainbows are very rare and your words are almost identical with those of the astronomer, Dr. A. M. Blodgett. Were you really in that railway accident when the ten-year-old boy saved a dozen lives?

Your account, by some strange coincidence, is almost word for word like a passage in a sermon by Rev. William Sunday.

I am brutally frank in saying that I don't believe that you have had one-tenth of the experiences that you claim. I am thus brutal because you ought to know that none of your hearers believe you either. And what are the psychological and spiritual effects of this pretense? They are altogether undesirable and perhaps even disastrous. Your people lose confidence in their minister. They are likely to say, " If he dissimulates in the pulpit, which ought to be a particularly sacred place for him, will he not falsify in some other places, or in all other places? "

What, then, can you do? Describe the lunar rainbow, if you need the illustration, but do not claim that you yourself have seen one. Tell about the train wreck if you must, but freely admit that you take the account from your reading. You will not lose oratorical effect and you will not lose the confidence of your parishioners or the respect of your own soul.

CASE III

Why Be Excruciating?

Dear Howard:

Just what do you expect to gain by introducing illustrations that for some of your people will be dreadful and agonizing? You presumably will gain their attention but you will not gain their favorable attention. Not thus, I think, will you gain their adherence or their salvation.

In two of your sermons you depict horrible cases of insanity. Do you remember that in the United States more patients are in mental hospitals than in all other hospitals combined and do you consider that it is altogether probable members of your congregation either have been victims of that awful misfortune or have near relatives who are now confined? Your points could be enforced just as well by illustrations that would not torture your hearers.

You speak of physical deformities. Have none of your parishioners cause to be sensitive about that subject? You speak of prisons. You speak of suicide. You speak of family disruption and disgrace. I do not say that such matters ought always to be ruled out of the pulpit, but I do advise you to be very, very careful about them and to use them with great reluctance.

I can see some of your best people cringe. I can see others nudge each other to signify that you have made a tactless blunder. Howard, you had better be merciful.

CASE IV

Bring on the Encyclopædia, Please!

Dear Felix:

You ask me to tell you frankly what I think of the illustrations in your convention sermon. As proof of your rather wide reading they were good. As helpful illustrations they were very poor.

What is an illustration for? It is to make thought clear. It is to make a somewhat difficult thought understandable. It is to make thought acceptable and potent. An illustration is like a window. What if the glass is so thick and dark that it absolutely shuts off the vision?

You must know very well that the people at that convention were not able to grasp the sense of some of those supposed illustrations. In fact, I doubt that any of us could. I couldn't, and I have studied some science myself.

Take this: " There is a celebrated experiment in which

a daguerreotype plate is ingeniously connected with a galvanometer, a gridiron of silver wires and a heart-registering helix, and then subjected to the action of light. The energy which was stored up in the sunbeam, when it darted in its long way from the central fires of the sun, is transformed by contact with the sensitive plate and resolved into several other modes of motion. For with its chemical action upon the plate there is produced electricity in the wires, magnetism in the coil, heat in the helix and molar motion in the needles of the index. The energy manifested in the solar beam is transformed into all the other modes of motion. And from that one radiate all the others."

That is fine when it is read and studied. It is thoroughly incomprehensible when it is heard in the midst of a sermon.

Here is this other one in regard to the latest method of breaking up the atom and extracting power for all the machinery of the world. Too technical, Felix, too technical! Never make your illustrations more difficult than the thought they are supposed to simplify. Never make your congregations wish for their encyclopædias.

CASE V

" A Certain Parishioner "

Dear Allan:

You are treading on dangerous ground when you speak, as you do in nearly all sermons, about " a certain parishioner " or " a member of my flock " or " a lady in perplexity."

A pastor in a great city, having thousands of constituents and millions of neighbors, may use those expressions without danger. You, however, are in a small community and are in your first pastorate.

It will not be difficult, therefore, for your nimble-witted hearers to identify the people about whom you preach. Can't you see Miss Harmon nudge her sister? And can't you see Mrs. Thornton exchange significant glances with Mrs. Williams? And can't you see " a certain parishioner " (poor, timid Mr. Roscoe, perhaps) grow red in the face and fidget about in extreme embarrassment?

Possibly your illustration has something to do with some folly, possibly with some sorrow, possibly with some deed of kindness. In any case it is undesirable to talk in public about some person who is present and will be recognized.

You can parallel the situation by thinking about a doctor. He may write a book and illustrate it by experiences in his own practice. If he has had many thousands of cases no harm will be done, but if he has had only a small country settlement he really will be divulging professional secrets.

If you feel that those illustrations are indispensable or even highly important rewrite them and delete the local references. Sensible? I think you will say so.

CASE VI

A Book Full of Illustrations

Dear Harvey:

When we took that long walk after your series of sermons at Pittsford, you asked me to suggest some books of illustrations. I would hesitate to do it for any young minister and I decline to do it for you. There is a danger that a preacher will depend on such volumes, will give a second-hand appearance to his sermons, will drag in illustrations that do not fit, or even will adjust his thought to fit what he finds in his book. In your own case you do not need anything of the kind. You are too fertile in your own mind and too keen in your study to allow anyone else to compile your material.

I will, however, recommend one book of illustrations, the best one in the world, one of which you already possess a good many copies, one from which you read every day of your life.

Why don't you use your Bible in your pulpit work? At Pittsford you drew illustrations from Shakespeare, Hugo, Tennyson, Tolstoy, Lincoln and many other authors; but not one did you introduce from the Book of Books. Why? The Bible is your treasure-house. To neglect it is like passing through an orchard laden with ripe and luscious fruit and gathering only the hard, misshapen windfalls.

I know that you are honest enough not to use interpolations, or mistranslations or misinterpretations. You need none of them to make the Scriptures effective.

Besides gaining the most forceful of illustrations for your subjects, you will find incidental and important advantages. You will help your people, who unfortunately do very little Bible reading, to become familiar with the world's supreme literature, and you will keep your own Biblical thought fresh and vital.

Now, just suppose. You had a sermon on " The Allies of the Christian Soldier." Suppose you had told the old story of Dothan. You had a sermon on " The Voice Within." Suppose you had related the incident of Peter and John, who said to the rulers, " Whether it be right in the sight of God to harken unto you more than unto God, judge ye." You had a sermon on " Christian Co-operation." Suppose you had thrilled your congregation with an account of the shipwrecked St. Paul who would not warm himself until he had brought his own bundle of sticks to the fire.

To call your attention to this matter ought to be sufficient. What you need is to cultivate the Bible habit.

Prayer to Precede Self-examination

God of All Grace, help me to speak Thy word with power.

May I present Thy truth with such clarity and such magnetism that through my faithful ministry many of Thy children may be brought to the beauty and the blessing of holiness.

Grant unto me ever fuller and fuller understanding of the laws of effective speech, to the end that I make Thy Gospel attractive to those whom I am privileged to influence.

I thank Thee for Thy call to Thy service.

SEARCHING SELF-EXAMINATION

(These questions are for no eyes but those of the minister himself. Each is to be considered thoughtfully, prayerfully and repeatedly.)

1. Have I been giving sufficient attention to effective homiletical illustration?

   Answer ....

2. Do I impress upon myself exactly what an illustration is for?

   Answer ....

3. Do I use too few illustrations and thus leave my sermons dull and dry?

   Answer ....

4. Do I use too many illustrations and thus make my sermons seem frothy and childish?

   Answer ....

5. Do my illustrations appear to be dragged in?

   Answer ....

6. Do I depend too much on books of illustrations?

Answer ....

7. Do I make a judicious use of good poems?

Answer ....

8. Do I relate as my own experiences of other men or of nobody?

Answer ....

9. Do I exaggerate without conscience?

Answer ....

10. Do I develop the art of figurative expression?

Answer ....

11. Do I make my illustrations as forceful as is proper?

Answer ....

12. Do I make my illustrations too hifalutin?

Answer ....

13. Do I introduce intricate and technical illustrations?

Answer ....

14. Are my illustrations too extended to be in proportion with the rest of my material?

Answer ....

15. Do I make use of old and outworn illustrations?

Answer ....

16. Do I tactlessly introduce local and personal illustrations that might embarrass members of the community?

Answer ....

17. Do I remember that the Bible is the world's greatest treasury of powerful illustrations?

Answer ....

18. Do I have some sufficient system for preserving my clippings and note-book references?

    Answer ....

19. Do I make sure that each illustration is appropriate for the particular sermon in which it is used?

    Answer ....

20. Do I repeat illustrations and thus give the impression that I have run out of fresh material?

    Answer ....

After considering all the suggested points, what ought I to do?

What *will* I do?

Prayer: Help me, O Heavenly Father, to keep my heart single for service and every day to gain some increase in the power to persuade.

SECTION EIGHT

THE VIRTUE OF VARIETY

(The professor, after examining a good many sermons by ex-students, in whose careers he is intensely interested, warns them against the deadly rut, and suggests ways of avoiding monotony.)

IN the old copy books at district schools boys and girls had to write over and over:

" Through all the course of this life, five things observe with
      care:
   Of whom you speak, to whom you speak, how, when and
      where."

A minister may well pin that injunction on his study
wall, simply substituting the word " preach " for the word
" speak." It is a prime mistake not to remember that
circumstances alter cases, places and faces. Every week
the preacher must try to fit his message to the exact needs
of the special people who are likely to be in his congregation. Only sermons that are carefully aimed can be expected to hit the mark. One pastor, wise from experience,
has, preceding every preparation, " a conference with
himself." That is, he sits down with paper and pencil and
asks himself a series of extremely important questions.
Some of them are: " Who probably will be at church next
Sunday? What special experiences have come to any of
my people? What sorrows? What temptations? What
good fortune? To what needs, as an understanding
friend, can I minister? How can I be helpful without
making it apparent that I am speaking of or for any
particular individuals? What community problems demand attention? What world events ought to be
discussed? How can I make this next sermon up-to-the-
minute? " No one ever accuses that minister of random
preaching.

CASE I

Rev. Mister Ditto

Classroom Number 6

Rev. Percy H. Messenger,
Auburn, California.

My dear Percy:
   You have sent me six sermons, all good, all very good
—and all on the same subject.

When I read the first one, I was delighted, albeit I had an impression that your line of thought was somewhat familiar. When I studied the second one, I was puzzled. And by the time I had finished the sixth one, I had passed through alarm to dismay. I had come to realize that in each one of these discourses you were preaching practically the same message with which you had so thrilled us all at the ordination of Tom Benedict.

You surely made a strong impression on that memorable evening. " Messenger is a man of might," declared Professor Grayson, expressing the universal verdict. Yet the reports that have come from your parish have been sadly disappointing, and in your letter you say that your congregations are small and are getting smaller.

These sermons reveal the probable explanation. You have become so enamored with a single phase of Christian thought that you preach nothing else and you have formed a homiletical habit that leads to extreme monotony. If you keep on, some wag in your church will dub you " Rev. Mister Ditto," and then your doom, so far as Auburn is concerned, will be sealed.

You and I are very fond of lobster—remember the old days at Buffini's! And we both are very fond of strawberry shortcake. Do you think, however, that either of us would care to eat lobster and strawberry shortcake three times a day and thirty days a month? At the Art Museum we used to enjoy the landscapes; but we would have been sorry if the galleries had contained no genre or other paintings. You know your psychology. You know the necessity of change for continued interest and developing impression.

Look closely at these submitted sermons. Here is one on the topic, " Apostles All," the text being, " Called to be an apostle." Your general idea is that any Christianity worthy of the name must make a man eager to share the gospel with others and to give it practical application in daily life. You specify that proper fields for apostolic speech and activity are the home, the church, the community and the nation. Capital! Your doctrine is sound and your presentation is powerful and persuasive. Another sermon is entitled "Gratitude in Action." You begin a little differently, but soon you are back on the same thesis and you swing around to Christianity in the home, the church, the community and the nation. Analyze the third, that called "The Greatest Thing in the World" and based on Drummond's booklet on First Corinthians, thirteen. After your charming introduction, you return to the same set of ideas. The same is true of your sermons on "Twentieth Century Courage," "Forward Be Our Watchword," and "Friends of Jesus." See how dreadfully you have narrowed your range of thought. Then think how the abundant gospel touches and illuminates and sanctifies every interest of mankind.

Any sermon of your group, taken alone, is excellent. A pulpit committee, hearing one, would be likely to give you a call. But to have them hear all six would be fatal.

Have you never known of the venerable Doctor Crossby, who always established a truth and then, in three divisions, considered it on the physical plane, the intellectual plane and the spiritual plane? He kept a few faithful hearers, who loved him for his paternal character, but who, knowing in advance what he was going to say, never took the trouble to listen to his sermons. In contrast, think of what everybody at Newbury says about your classmate, Blanchard, "We have to attend every Sunday, for we never know what he is going to say, though we are sure that it will be something worth hearing."

Now, what are you to do to deliver yourself from the bondage of monotony?

When you have recognized your fault, you will have gone far toward its correction, for whenever you begin preparation of a sermon a kind monitor from your subconscious mind will say, "Is this, except for a different text and an altered phraseology, the same message that you gave last Sunday and the Sunday before and the Sunday before that?" And you will decline to duplicate.

You will be wise to plan your homiletical program far ahead. Make out a list of subjects upon which you expect to preach, forcing yourself to seek wide variety. If you wait until the day of actual preparation before thinking of a subject and then expect something to "pop into your head," you are likely to discover that the same old theme, only slightly disguised, will pop week after week.

Classify your sermons. At the beginning of a season, make out a calendar, with an approximate number of discourses on each of the principal phases of your preaching; for instance, the number on applied Christianity, on textual interpretation, on systematic theology, on special days, on church life, on spiritual reinforcements, and so on. I do not mean, of course, that you ought to decide the particular dates a year in advance, or that you ought to follow slavishly any program of subjects. I do mean that you ought to use some such device to keep your sense of proportion. After preaching, enter your sermon according to its class, so that a glance at your record will enable you to check up on your own practice.

Vary your homiletic method, being even radical enough to depart if necessary from some of the rules that you learned in Classroom Number 6. To this end, study the sermons of other ministers. Study them, not to plagiarize, of course, but to impress upon yourself that there are many truths included in your great truth and that there are many methods of approach, development and application.

The other night I was at Professor Herring's, and his small Jack turned on the victrola. I was pleased to listen to an exquisite rendering of "The Spring Song." Evidently the youngster agreed that that was a fine selection, for when it was finished he immediately turned back the record and began it again. He repeated it over and over, until it became torture to everyone else. His mother besought him to try another selection, but you know how very limited is his mother's influence. When I left, he was still playing "The Spring Song," and he gave no signs of desisting. Percy, I wonder why it was that that unfortunate experience made me think of you.

My dear friend, you have power to be a master in the ministry. Deliver yourself from the thralldom of ditto.

Yours for progress in vision and service,

The Pedagogue Homiletical.

CASE II

"Here Comes Pegasus"

Dear Peter:

You evidently are very fond of poetry. Good!

I must compliment you, moreover, upon your wise judgment in selecting for your sermons such poems as your hearers can readily understand. Bishop Poltham used to quote often from the great classics, but the passages were such as ought to be read and reread in order to be appreciated, as, for instance, parts of Browning's "Paracelsus." It may be that his hearers were impressed by his erudition but they were not enlightened or inspired. You, introducing the simpler works of minor poets, are far more helpful.

But, why so many poems? I note that you always close with one and that in almost every division of almost every sermon you quote one or more. Fine as are the thoughts and attractive as are the expressions, that is too much of a good thing. Those high-school students, I fear, sit nudging each other and whispering, "Now it's about time for Pegasus." Do you wonder that they, and perhaps their elders, smile when Pegasus promptly wings his way to keep his appointment?

CASE III

" A Walking Dictionary "

Dear Carlton:

Hamlet spoke disparagingly of " words, words, words." It is said, however, that Shakespeare had the greatest vocabulary of any human being. A savage never acquires more than a few hundred words, using the same ones over and over, his ideas being general and foggy.

A modern preacher may not hope to be a Shakespeare, but he ought not to be content to be a savage. A limited use of language may not indicate a narrow range of thought but it is likely to do so. The use of many terms, with nice distinction in definition, makes for intellectual activity and development.

To some of the boys I am urging variety in subject, but that does not seem to be your especial need. Variety in expression, however, would give you literary charm and pulpit power. Listening to this sermon on " Spiritual Calisthenics," a person might say, " How this man repeats his ideas! " A careful reading shows that such is not your fault, but rather a repetition of phraseology. Take that one word " calisthenics." How many times do you suppose that you have used it? I counted twenty-four on the first few pages and then desisted. There are good synonyms, are there not?

There are certain definite efforts that, having recognized your need, you can make for vocabulary enlargement. Cultivate an enthusiasm and love for words. Study their derivation and history. Carefully distinguish between them. In reading, note the new terms that you see and, without forcing, adopt those that seem to fit into your mental processes. In writing, make a conscious effort for variety. Avoid the line of least resistance, which may be to repeat and repeat. A book of synonyms and antonyms, if used intelligently, will be helpful. Own the latest edition of *Roget's Thesaurus*. Buy a good book, not too technical, on linguistics.

I know a man who has labored diligently for many years to develop his English—and has gained his reward. There is nothing pedantic or offensively pretentious about his utterance, but it is now a matter of course for him to speak with precision and variety. The students call him " a walking dictionary." How would you like to improve your speech until someone should call you by such a name?

CASE IV

The Occasional

Dear Alonzo:

So the program committee gave you a great honor! It was fine that at the annual Conference you should preach " the occasional sermon." I do not recall that such a distinction ever before was conferred on so young a minister, and, as you know, my memory goes back over a good many years.

This manuscript on " Crises " shows that you appreciated your privilege and rose to your opportunity. Well done, my friend!

I have been wondering, however, why any sermon ever should miss being " occasional." Every Sunday morning is a special occasion for any preacher who keeps in touch with his people and holds them sympathetically in his heart of hearts. There never is a day when someone down there in the pews does not have some particular joy or sorrow, or temptation, or pain, or problem. There never is a day when there is not a need for the message of God to give a specific gospel.

New occasions always! And

"New occasions teach new duties;
Time makes ancient good uncouth."

CASE V

The Exciter

Dear Christopher:

In your letter you forestall the criticism that you expect me to make on your sermons. Knowing that in the classroom I urge variety in preaching and recognizing that your work is all along similar lines, you say, "But, Professor, what can I do, except to preach the only ideas that pop into my head?"

Well, son, if the same idea continues to pop to the exclusion of all others, you had better send out a very urgent invitation for some strangers to come and break up the monopoly.

You may get a suggestion in an electric power station. I went into one the other day and I was awe-filled as I looked at the gigantic whirring, whirling armatures. Down in a corner I saw a busy little contrivance, so diminutive by comparison that it made me laugh. "What is that tiny fellow doing down there?" I asked. "Is that just a miniature put in for exhibition?" "No," said the attendant, "that little chap is highly important, in fact, indispensable. That is the *exciter*. We have to get that started first and then capture from it the impulse that sets in motion all these giants."

It is often necessary for a man who hopes to enlarge his thought to have an exciter. If the sluggish brain shows a reluctance to abandon old, familiar channels its owner may get himself into a creative mood by judicious reading. This does not mean that he expects to plagiarize—far from it. It means that his cerebral substance is to be stirred for fresh and original activity.

Different men respond to different forms of awakening literature. A great metropolitan preacher finds himself ready for composition after reading a chapter of some absorbing detective story. In extreme contrast think of Doctor Burlingham, who reads in the Psalms. Doctor Crane, as long as he lived, resorted to Dickens. One of our young ministers, not a Communist, dips for a few minutes into Karl Marx.

You ask about my own practice. That's fair. Almost any part of the Bible will start my wheels. In secular literature I find nothing more stimulating than a chapter from *Sartor Resartus* or a poem by Walt Whitman.

CASE VI

Sermonic Elasticity

Dear George:

Twenty-one pages apiece! In delivery, I presume, about twenty-five minutes apiece! What a strange coincidence that your six sermons should be so uniform in length! Is there some rule in your conscious mind or in your subconscious mind demanding that a sermon shall be never shorter and never longer?

To me that seems mechanical and undesirable. It reminds me of one of the pastors in the church of my childhood. There was a clock on the side wall and this worthy man always dragged along until exactly seven minutes before twelve. Then the Bible was closed with a bang, a hymn was announced, and the congregation, roused and relieved, rose to its feet. How many eyes watched that clock! The preacher's eyes! The children's eyes! And, if the truth must be told, the deacons' eyes!

It does seem as though the nature of your themes would demand variety in length. One subject may be so simple that a brief statement, illustration, application are all that is necessary. Another may require much elucidation, elaboration and, perhaps, exhortation.

I know what you will say. You will remind me that your people want to leave the church at a certain minute in order to catch their busses and get home for Sunday dinners. All right. Then, can you not adapt the rest of your service so that the whole will fill practically the usual limits? If you are to preach thirty-five minutes you can have shorter readings and fewer hymns, while if you are to preach but twenty minutes you can allow yourself and your musicians an elaborate preliminary program. That's the way Doctor Granger manages.

CASE VII

"Days Like These"

Dear Levi:

You are to be congratulated. You are to be congratulated upon living in a great era, on preaching at a time when the Christian Church faces an unprecedented opportunity and a supreme responsibility. Crisis! "Civilization at the Crossroads!" "Christianity at the Crossroads!"

In all my long life I never have known a time when there has been such need for a vital and vitalizing message. Alas for humanity distraught!

Levi, what are you doing in "days like these"? Are you asleep? Are you contented to leave your people asleep?

Here are half a dozen sermons which might have been respectable, even excellent, ten years ago. They are very calm discourses. They treat of ordinary duties of ordinary men in ordinary times. Today they are not worthy of your ability or your character. Wake up, dear boy, and give us some stirring words that show that you know when and where you are living. I want you to help save your country, your Church, and your civilization.

PRAYER TO PRECEDE SELF-EXAMINATION

God of the Gospel, help me to understand something of the height and depth and breadth of the Christian message.

May I ever remember that it is sufficient in all the exigencies of human life and for men of all sorts and conditions.

Remembering the excellencies of Thy truth, may I never be narrow in thought or monotonous in my utterance.

SEARCHING SELF-EXAMINATION

(These questions are for no eyes but those of the minister himself. Each is to be considered thoughtfully, prayerfully and repeatedly.)

1. Am I in danger of deadly monotony in subject or expression?

   Answer ....

2. Have I been falling into any homiletical rut?

   Answer ....

3. Do I make out a sermonic calendar, insuring variety throughout the year?

   Answer ....

4. Do I ever study the sermons of other men for the specific purpose of observing how they secure freshness of thought and development?

   Answer ....

5. Do I introduce good poems into my sermons?

   Answer ....

6. Do I introduce too many?

Answer ....

7. Do I have the poems at the same approximate points in all sermons?

Answer ....

8. Do I classify my sermons?

Answer ....

9. If so, in what categories?

Answer ....

10. Are my sermons always divided and subdivided according to the same system?

Answer ....

11. Am I making a constant effort to enlarge my working vocabulary?

Answer ....

12. Do I remember the advantage of using good synonyms?

Answer ....

13. Do I regard every sermon as " occasional "?

Answer ....

14. Do I read for the purpose of attaining a creative mood?

Answer ....

15. What authors help me most to original thinking?

Answer ....

16. Do I give the Bible a fair chance for intellectual stimulation and spiritual exhilaration?

    Answer ....

17. Are my sermons of uniform length?

    Answer ....

18. Would it be well for me to have more "sermonic elasticity" and to adjust the other parts of my service accordingly?

    Answer ....

19. Do I realize that great national and international crises are upon us?

    Answer ....

20. Do I know that in these days of dire distress and danger my people look to me for special comfort and guidance?

    Answer ....

After considering all the suggested points, what ought I to do?

What *will* I do?

Prayer: O God, in whose service I gladly re-enlist, grant to me ever increasing vision and constant power to present Thy Gospel in fresh forms and figures and with new magnetism.

SECTION NINE

A GOOD SERMON DESERVES—

(Rev. Williston Hervey and other young ministers have
sent manuscript sermons to their professor, expecting that
he will criticize them from the standpoints of construction,
language, illustration and the like. Having heard them
preach, however, he thinks that they need suggestions, not
so much about sermon making as about sermon delivery.
He writes to them as one who loves them and is eager to
have them do their most and utmost for the Kingdom.)

STUDENTS had a stock question, which, in his later
years, they liked to ask their beloved Doctor Hammond.
" Teacher," they would say, " which do you prefer, a poor
sermon well delivered or a good sermon poorly delivered? " " Young men," he would answer, with flashing
eyes, " I refuse to consider such a question. God demands good sermons well delivered and no respectable
preacher is satisfied with anything less! " The dear
veteran had a right to say that, for in all his long life no
one knew him to preach a poor sermon or deliver his message without enthusiasm and power.

CASE I

" I Hereby Convey "

Classroom Number 6

Rev. Williston Hervey,
New Roxbury, Indiana.

My dear Williston:

I beg of you to convey something.

The sermons that you have submitted have many excellencies, and, indeed, are so good that I shall postpone
the minor homiletical criticisms that might be made.

I want to talk about another matter, repeating advice often but unsuccessfully reiterated while you were in school. You seem to lack the fundamental idea of *delivery*.

You have animation. Your voice is loud enough, you prance enough, you pound enough. You abound in the well-known " wim, wigor and witality."

Yet, somehow, you do not deliver. At Charlestown, at Deven and at Pullman your audiences were inattentive and uninspired. How dreadful it must be to shout and shout and yet know that the people are not listening!

You say, " What lack I yet? " You need to think out the real definition of " delivery." You will decide that (a) there should be someone to give, (b) something to be given, and (c) someone to receive. Now take those three simple facts into the pulpit.

There must be somebody to give. You are that highly honored person. Think over and over of your glorious privilege as an apostle, an evangelist, a spokesman for Christ, a messenger for the Most High.

There must be something to be given. What a treasure you have to convey—" the glorious Gospel of the blessed God "! Yours to impart is the truth that shall make men free. Yours to share is the religion that leads men to the more abundant life.

There must be somebody to receive. Think of your listeners as individuals, not as " the general public." Your audience is made up of men and women, boys and girls, each one with very serious problems, each one with temptations, each one with heavy burdens. You know their needs, for as a pastor you carry them always on your heart. When you preach let it be to real people, not as to straw people, dehumanized into a " general public."

With these three facts burned into your consciousness, you will remember that the delivery of a sermon is more than " speaking a piece," more than declaiming, more than oratory, more than elocution. (It is said that our

Doctor Woodruff is the author of the story about the little girl who defined elocution as the way in which in some states criminals are put to death.) You must be as eager as the lawyer before a jury. Yes, I should think much more eager.

Think about delivery in some other fields. You are an athlete. What would have happened to you if, when you were the college pitcher, you failed really to deliver the ball? A business man sends out an auto loaded with goods. What would happen to the driver if he neglected to deliver that merchandise? A general entrusts to a subordinate a most important message. What would happen to that soldier if he failed to deliver that order? You know Elbert Hubbard's " Message to Garcia." Read it next Sunday before you go into the pulpit. Remember that you are under command and that your Leader expects delivery.

You may ask for specific help.

First, *think* it at them. Develop the sense of mental contact with those people in the pews—just as you do in the most earnest conversation. The best teachers of public address emphasize that a speaker's work must be *from the mind side*. For the time being forget your gesture. Let gesture be the natural expression of your intense thought. For the time being forget your voice. Let the variations of voice follow inevitably your intense thought.

Secondly, *love* it at them. Here is where your delivery may differ from that of a scientific lecturer or a political orator. Their concerns are with matters, important no doubt, but not so important as the *cure of souls*. As a minister, you hold those people with ardent Christian affection and that affection should give carrying power to every word. Phillips Brooks was said to magnetize his hearers. How? By loving them into the truth.

What you need is to burn into your soul the convictions that your gospel is supremely important, that your listeners are supremely important, and that, as a conveyer of saving truth, you are a supremely blessed man.

Paul declared, " Woe is me, if I preach not the gospel." Can you imagine him as perfunctory in thought or in-effective in delivery?

In our town we have two preachers, one of whom makes much noise with little effect and one of whom makes little noise with much effect. Noise or no noise, I want you to be powerful in conveyance. Your sermons are good and a good sermon deserves—a good delivery.

> Yours for power through the spirit,
>
> The Pedagogue Homiletical.

CASE II

D. D.

Dear Wilbur:

A visitor came to the theological school and, after listening to a sermon by one of our young hopefuls, said to a professor, " That lad has possibilities but you ought to give him the D. D."

" Isn't it a little early for that honor? " he was asked.

" Not a day too soon," he replied, " for in this case I mean *daily dynamite*."

The theologue had worked long and hard and had pro-duced a very excellent sermon, one that might have stirred and vastly influenced a congregation. Apparently, however, he was not stirred himself, and his listless de-livery robbed a notable discourse of all possible useful-ness.

The sequel? You would be surprised if I should con-fide to you the name of that young preacher. Now, after two decades, he is known as one of the strongest, most vital, most thrilling speakers in our fellowship. I heard him last month and I thought, " Brother, somehow you must have found a good supply of dynamite, for you act as though you had a double dose every day!"

Wilbur, my boy, do you know of any supply house where *you* could lay in a liberal supply of that explosive? Do not be offended if I say that you are in tragic need of oratorical dynamite—or even TNT.

These sermons that you have sent me are delightful. What possibilities you have! What insight into the deep problems of human life and divine grace! What felicity of expression! What patness and power in illustration! I do not wonder that one of your contributions was selected for publication in that magazine of national renown.

Why is it that you do not succeed in any of your parishes? I have heard you repeatedly, and I think it is because, while your sermons are good, you deliver them as though they were "no good." Not by voice, not by gesture, not by facial expression, do you give a hint that you think your message is of any great importance to you or to your people. I wonder if you ever thank God for your truth and for your unspeakable privilege of sharing it with sin-sick men and women.

Do you remember Doctor McArthur's world-famous epigram? He said, "The great need of the Church is to make indifferent people different." Why are you indifferent to the Gospel of Christ? You had better recall the words of the apostle, "It is good to be affected zealously always in a good thing."

Why do you give such an impression of lassitude when you are in the pulpit? Is the cause physical? I don't think so. If it is you had better see a competent physician.

Is the cause psychical? Presumably so. You lack what the crossword puzzlers call *élan*. Perhaps you have an inferiority complex. Perhaps you have a subconscious horror of oratorical display. Perhaps you never have thought seriously about this duty of conveying your truth. Perhaps you take undue pride in your compositions and think that they need no particular delivery.

At any rate you need a thorough self-examination and perhaps a new consecration.

I advise you to practice before your mirror, not restraining your fervor. And I advise you to have a good session with yourself every Sunday just before you pass from your study into the auditorium. I assume, as a matter of course, that you do pray at that time. In addition, give yourself a strong mental treatment. Say, " I have something precious to give; I have something *very* precious to give; I have something *very, very* precious to give, and I am going to give it with power ! "

Then, perhaps, you had better sing to yourself:

> " Awake, my soul, stretch every nerve
> And preach with vigor on."

CASE III

Fifty Fifty

Dear Jefferson:

A strong manuscript is only fifty per cent of a sermon, perhaps less than fifty per cent.

One of our men was called to the Pacific Coast. I am not at liberty to give you his name, but you have met him.

He applied for a vacant pulpit out there and, at the request of the board of governors, sent on some sample sermons, eight or ten of them. Good sermons they were to read, and on the strength of them he was engaged.

Then came a sad experience for the parish and for the man, for those governors found that the minister who can write is not necessarily the minister who can deliver. This preacher's sermons, excellent in thought and composition, were dead when given from the pulpit. He failed utterly because he could not deliver what, with diligent labor, he had worked out.

I cite this case to you, Jefferson, because you are in danger of disappointment for the same reason. I have read your manuscripts with deep satisfaction and I have heard you preach three times with intense grief. Wake up, dear lad! Give your people the other fifty per cent.

I am glad to say that your brother minister was wise enough to learn his lesson. He came back to this vicinity, took a neighboring parish, and re-entered our school for special drill in the department of public speech. To use his own inelegant but effective expression, he " got his dander up." Today he not only writes great sermons but he delivers them greatly.

You could not return for postgraduate work. You could, however, do much for yourself. Read some books on speaking. Observe how other men succeed. Have a private teacher if you can. Practice, practice, practice! At any rate, be intensely interested in convincing and converting your people. Remember that you are paid for 100 per cent sermons.

CASE IV

" Dear Corner "

Dear Clifford:

Is there someone, invisible to most of us, perched in the upper right-hand corner of your auditorium? When I visited your church two weeks ago, I noticed that you did not once look at the people in the pews but seemed to address all your sermon to someone about thirty feet over their heads. You had written a good sermon, but you seemed woefully lacking in the sense of direction.

In conversation you expect a man to " look you straight

in the eye." If he fails to do so, you suspect that he is shifty in spirit and character. What, then, should parishioners think of a minister who seems afraid honestly and frankly to face them?

I am going to tell you something. When I was a student I had your habit in an extreme form. I suppose I was diffident. At any rate, I never looked at my audience. It was my good fortune to have a course in public speaking with a man who did not think that he was paid to spare the feelings of his pupils. In a voice to shake the rafters he would interrupt me. "Who is out that window?" he would shout. Or, "Who is up there on the ceiling?" Or, "Unless you will speak to *me*, down here, the recitation is over!" He startled me and angered me, but his training was worth thousands of dollars.

I wish that you could have some work with such a teacher as that. He could multiply your effectiveness, not merely by two but by ten. The chairman of your Board of Trustees said to me, "You sent us a young man with a lot of bright ideas, but he never seems to preach to us; instead, he seems to be trying to convert a spot away up on the right-hand corner."

Speak to *somebody*, Clifford. *Eyes are made to talk with.*

CASE V

Stress and Distress

Dear Westbrook:

Come over to my study some time and I will show you some manuscripts written a hundred years before those that you have sent. There are several interesting facts about them in addition to a theology that you never have preached and never have heard preached. One fact is that men in those days spent time on penmanship, every minute letter in this rather effeminate hand being as perfect as though from copper plate. Another is that he knew his Bible and interpreted it with absolute literalism.

A third fact is that the author was thoughtful, not only of his handwriting and his doctrine but of his emphasis in delivery. How can we tell that? All through he has underlined some words, double underlined some and even triple underlined some others. And in some places on the margin he has written, " Thunder here." So far as I can judge, he planned to thunder in the proper places!

Ah, if all through human life we could understand the art of emphasis, what a fine world this would be! Poor, mistaken mortals, however, we are always slighting the greatest things and underscoring those of petty and passing moment. Poor little Grace was unspeakably distressed today when she broke a five-cent saucer! We all put last things first and first things last.

Public speakers need to be very careful about stress. Else they may say something very different from what they intend. " *What* is man that thou art mindful of him? " " What *is* man that thou art mindful of him? " " What is *man* that thou art mindful of him? " " What is man that *thou* art mindful of him? " " What is man that thou *art* mindful of him? " " What is man that thou art *mindful* of him? " " What is man that thou art mindful of *him?* " See how a slight change in emphasis can alter the whole effect of a passage.

Take the first verse of the Twenty-third Psalm. Throw your emphasis first on " Lord," then on " is," then on " my," then on " shepherd." See?

I think that some men never read their Scripture lessons in advance, for in passage after passage they fail to bring out the real meaning of the author. And in reading from their own manuscripts they seem to do themselves a similar disservice.

Well, Westbrook, *you* are one of those men. The sermons that you gave at Burlington were well conceived and well written but they were not well delivered. What an injustice to yourself! What an injustice to your listeners! What an injustice to the Christian Church!

What did you mean when you said, " The godly have *laid* up treasures in Heaven " instead of " The godly have laid up treasures in *heaven* "? What did you mean when you said, " When the Prodigal *came* to himself " instead of " When the Prodigal came to *himself* "?

Evidently it is your intention to take your manuscripts into the pulpit and to read them nearly word for word. That is all right. Some men are not intended for extemporaneous preachers and it is possible for them to be extremely effective even if " confined to notes." If you are to read, however, read with care, demanding of yourself the proper amount of emphasis and the proper placing of emphasis.

What a delight it is to hear Joseph Fort Newton preach! Marvellous vocabulary? Certainly. But every word made powerful by exactly the right weight of emphasis.

Why have you fallen into a slipshod habit of delivery? Largely because no sincere friend has spoken to you with entire frankness. Now a sincere friend has spoken to you with entire frankness. Another reason is that you have not watched yourself. Henceforth watch yourself.

CASE VI

Triumphantly FinISH

Dear Clyde:

My young grandson likes to blow up a rubber balloon and then allow the air to escape. You know the process and the effect. At the first release the current rushes out as though to fill the world, then it comes more and more slowly; at the end the poor plaything simply falls over, limp and weak.

Some ministers are like that in their delivery. Every sentence is begun with strength and apparently ended with exhaustion.

You remember what Florence told me at Baldwin. You felt both hurt and pleased to have her criticize you before your old professor. It is not pleasant for any of us to have our faults openly stated, but you knew that you had a first-class wife and that she was seeking only your own good. Now that I have heard you preach I see that her words were well founded. She said, " March and Clyde come in like a lion and go out like a lamb."

Looking over your manuscripts, I observe that all your sentences are formed in accordance with rhetorical rules. Every one begins well and ends with the most important phrase. The effect on the reader is one of carrying power.

If you were consistent you would apply the same psychological good sense in your delivery. But you do not. Your voice wanes. At the end of each sentence it drops away to nothingness. You seem like a runner who puts all his strength in the first lap and faints before the race is finished.

YOU BEGIN WITH POWER BUT YOU PETER OUT and fade aw . . . . . .

I think the explanation is that you have a subconscious impression that because the thought is complete in your own mind it must be complete in that of the listener. You have thought your thought and you do not realize that you have failed to say your say.

Now, what is the effect? It may be that you give the suggestion of physical weakness, as though you lacked the stamina to carry through. Or it may be that you give the suggestion of doubt as to the real worth of your statement. At any rate, you lose the dynamic effect of a clear utterance with the climax at the end.

You ask for advice. Mere recognition of your fault will go far toward its cure. One young preacher simply watched himself and soon conquered the costly habit. It may be that you can practice with a good teacher. Who? Perhaps you will find in your own neighborhood some competent professor of the spoken word. Possibly, however, under your own roof you may find someone who will help you without money and without price. Florence really *is* a fine young woman, isn't she? Why not let her help?

The lady of my heart has just been listening by benefit of the radio to a symphony concert. I have heard enough to notice that each of the beautiful classic selections comes to a glorious, triumphant close. The composers can teach us ministers.

PRAYER TO PRECEDE SELF-EXAMINATION

O God, who hast called me to Thy apostleship, bless me as a seeker for truth and as a giver of truth.

Banish from my heart all foolish fear. If Thou art for me, who can be against me?

Purge from my heart all selfish ambition and help me with singleness of purpose to speak Thy saving word.

SEARCHING SELF-EXAMINATION

(These questions are for no eyes but those of the minister himself. Each is to be considered thoughtfully, prayerfully and repeatedly.)

1. Do I remember that composing a sermon may be only half or less than half of my responsibility regarding it?

   Answer ....

2. In preaching do I simply "go through" my sermon or do I really have the thought of *delivering* a precious gift?

   Answer ....

3. Do I understand and sufficiently give thanks for my privilege as a messenger?

   Answer ....

4. Do I speak as eagerly and earnestly to a congregation as a lawyer does to a jury?

   Answer ....

5. Do I have the mental attitude of one who " speaks for a verdict "?

   Answer ....

6. In preaching do I keep myself duly impressed with the dignity and importance of my message?

   Answer ....

7. In preaching do I consider my hearers as needing and beloved individuals rather than as " general public "?

   Answer ....

8. Do I " think it at them "?

   Answer ....

9. Do I " love it at them "?

   Answer ....

10. Do I, like the young man, need " D. D."?

    Answer ....

11. Have I an inferiority complex that restrains my delivery?

    Answer ....

12. Do I think my sermons so good that delivery seems of little importance?

    Answer ....

13. Am I afraid that someone will accuse me of oratorical display?

Answer ....

14. Do I address the ceiling and the corners instead of the congregation?

Answer ....

15. If so, why?

Answer ....

16. Do I talk with my eyes?

Answer ....

17. Am I careful to emphasize what is truly important?

Answer ....

18. Am I careful to end my sentences so that the thought is carried with power?

Answer ....

19. Do I read good books on public speaking?

Answer ....

20. Could I arrange for private lessons on delivery?

Answer ....

After considering all the suggested points, what ought I to do?

What *will* I do?

Prayer: For the marvellous power of speech, my Heavenly Father, I thank Thee. In its use may I never be apathetic or careless. May I increase every day in power to do Thy work and proclaim Thy word.

SECTION TEN

"SPEAK THE SPEECH, I PRAY YOU"

(The professor, having studied the sermons sent to him by several former students, still his "boys" to him, decides that his criticisms are needed, not particularly regarding the discourses, but much more regarding presentation. Having listened to the young men at various places, he is disturbed about their ineffectual delivery.)

OLD Doctor Birmingham used to insist that his theologues were all angels. He used the word in the New Testament sense as signifying a messenger from God and he urged the boys never to forget their divine commission or its implications. His practice gave a good deal of fun to him, to the students and to the general public. Alas, he taught a good many neophytes who did not seem quite angelic in ability, ideals or conduct! He had an idea there, however, that was vastly beneficial to some quite inefficient young speakers. His exhortations delivered them from many a foolish notion and lazy practice. " Now, remember that you are an angel! Carry yourself like an emissary from the Most High! Utter—don't mutter! Utter—don't stutter! Your message is worthy of a clear, strong voice! Don't swallow your gospel! Be a first-rate angel!" And so on. Thus young fellows with dubious prospects became successful " angels " because the good doctor persistently reminded them of their heavenly message.

CASE I

" An Organ with a Thousand Stops "

Classroom Number 6

Rev. Oliver H. Hearst,
Dartmouth, Tennessee.

My dear Oliver:

It is said that Ralph Waldo Emerson had an " irresistible voice." When he addressed lyceum audiences he captured them, partly by his message, partly by his gracious personality, but largely by his marvellous voice. Some called it angelic.

As you know, we have in our own fellowship a minister of similar power. He is Doctor Hazelman, with whom, fortunately, you have had some intimate associations. Mrs. Seaton, in her recent book, says that his voice " is like an organ with a thousand stops." She also speaks of it as " a gift of God."

Not long ago I had the privilege of assisting at a service in his church and I learned some interesting facts. In his study, a half hour before we entered the pulpit, he began lightly to sing. I was surprised, for he is no musician. Then he recited stanzas from Poe's poem, " The Bells." For full five minutes he rang those bells in all the various moods suggested by the great master. " The bells, bells, bells, bells, bells."

" Don't you do this? " he asked.

I shook my head.

" You ought to; you ought to do this or something similar. Your young men ought to. Every minister ought to."

He then practiced with other words like " tools," " calls," " sighs," " tease," and " muse." I could have smiled to see that eminent man going through those apparently childish exercises, but it was no joking matter to him.

There was no time for conversation just then, but in the afternoon I asked him about his practice.

" My voice is not a gift of God," he said; " at least not a free gift. When, as a young man, I came into this ministry from another denomination the leaders told me that I had better not try to preach, as my voice was so unusually poor. I decided to ' show them.' I thought about the patient preparation that a public singer has to make and I concluded that the privilege of preaching the Gospel was great enough to warrant any possible sacrifice. I accepted my handicap as a challenge and for thirty-five years I have been trying to make my voice fit to proclaim the grace of God."

He told me also about an acquaintance of his, a lawyer, who worked just as hard along the same line.

Now, Oliver, you ought to take this right home. I have told you a good many times, in school and out, that you ought to give your voice careful and constant training. It is not the worst voice in the world, but it might be much better. It is high-pitched and it is husky. It prevents you from gaining more than fifty per cent of your possible success and usefulness. My own son Jack needs this same advice, I am sorry to say, but I cannot induce him to do anything about it. The same is true of Wilson. Vincent Davis is remarkably blessed by nature, but even he could gain by practice.

Isn't it strange that a man will work all the week trying to prepare effective sermons and then will neglect the instrument with which he is to deliver them! And your manuscripts show that you have worked hard. But, having heard you twice on recent occasions, I can see no vocal gains.

What ought you to do? First, consecrate your larynx. I mean that definitely and seriously. Just as you consecrate your hands to do God's work and your feet to run

God's errands, consecrate your larynx and all your vocal organs to speak His word. The invigoration of your utterance will seem marvellous.

I will make just a very few other suggestions. One is that you use that very poem, "The Bells." If it has helped Dr. Hazelman it ought to help you. I have adopted it, even at my age, and it has helped me. Another point: Fill your lungs over and over, perhaps for three or five minutes, before you go to the platform. By filling them I do not mean merely the upper lungs, but the lower lungs, "away down in your boots," where the air seldom penetrates. Then, there is the practice of inhaling some weak but good germicide before beginning your service. I find that it clears the air passages and I wouldn't go to church without my little bottle.

These simple suggestions, *very* simple, may help a little, but you ought to have help from someone besides a professor of homiletics. You ought to have a thorough course, covering months or years. You ought to read good books on the subject and you ought to have the guidance of a first-class professional teacher. Then, of course, you should be prayerfully faithful to his instructions.

> Faithfully and vocally yours,
> The Pedagogue Homiletical.

CASE II

More for Oliver

Dear Oliver:

You are like your namesake, made immortal by Mr. Dickens. In school days you were always asking for second helpings, thus greatly pleasing the faculty, and now you request more hints regarding your vocal culture.

I'll tell you about a lifelong custom of Doctor Gregory,

who has one of the finest voices and one of the most effective deliveries in our ministry. He says that his power
has come from reading to Mrs. Gregory. In their early
days together he read aloud *Les Miserables* (Battle of
Waterloo and all) and he has followed that with hundreds
of volumes, both classic and transient.

At first he read to her for her pleasure but he soon
found that he himself was receiving the greatest benefit.
Upon my recommendation several of our young ministers
are trying the Gregory experiment, much to the edifica-
tion of their wives and much to the improvement of their
vocal organs. Oliver, you had better join their number.

CASE III

Sunday Morning Nutrition

Dear Eric:

You have asked me about your delivery, saying that
you seem to lack the necessary *élan*. I think that in your
case the trouble is not psychical but physical. Ministers
have some queer notions about their Sunday morning
breakfasts—and the Kingdom suffers in consequence.
Parson A goes into his pulpit suffering from malnutrition,
Parson B goes into his suffering from under-nutrition, and
Parson C goes into his suffering from over-nutrition. You
may say that every man is a problem by himself and that
no general rule can be laid down. I will venture the general rule that every man ought to give this highly important matter most serious thought, probably with wise
counsel from an experienced physician.

If I were to advise you offhand I would say that you
ought to eat on Sunday morning a good, nourishing meal
and that you ought to eat it early enough so that it will
be well digested before you begin your strenuous pulpit
work. To gorge oneself just before preaching, as some

ministers do, is probably a sin against the Christian Church—an institution that has a right to demand that its spokesmen shall be at their best. Gorging is one extreme and starving is the other.

Your dear wife has confided to my dear wife, "My Eric never eats any breakfast on Sunday morning." I thought so. I thought so each of the three Sundays that I heard you preach at Edmonds. You seemed weak and uncomfortable. You were pale. You trembled. You lacked driving power behind your utterance. Where did you pick up that heretical whim? My prescription, humbly given, is: a good breakfast, a little heavier than usual and a little earlier than usual.

CASE IV

A Word That Costs

Dear Stanley:

What is the most frequent word in your public addresses? No doubt you will reply quickly and confidently, "Why, it is the word ' the.' " After listening to you on four recent occasions I have the impression that there is another word, thoroughly undesirable, that you use oftener than even the definite article. I refer to the word " er." Perhaps that isn't a word, but, at any rate, it is something that you insert in almost every sentence.

" Now, er, is the time, er, er, for every good man, er, to come, er, to the service of, er, his party."

Cruel exaggeration? Some overstatement, perhaps, but no intentional cruelty.

You remember how impatient old Doctor Hawkins used to get when a student hemmed and hawed over a sentence. Sometimes he would exclaim, " If you have anything to say, young man, out with it! " Frankly, I have felt like crying thus when I have been in your congregation. Your hesitation gets on my nerves, which is not important, and it gets on the nerves of your parishioners, which is vastly important.

You are not alone in your " ers " and your " ahs." Thousands of public speakers are guilty of the same dreadful practice. Oh, what a cost! Their platform and pulpit efficiency is cut in two or worse.

And what is the explanation? Just habit in most cases. With some men it is the result of nervousness, a trouble which they could overcome by effort and prayer. With others it is caused by low vitality, either physical or intellectual.

At any rate, it is one of the curses of the Christian Church. You, strong of body and mind, and with a great message to deliver, ought to be forthright and powerful in utterance.

Read Hamlet's address to the players, " Speak the speech, I pray thee." Indeed, you may well use it as an exercise in delivery.

CASE V

Exterminate the Frogs

Dear Francis:

The dictionary says that a " frog in the throat " is a slight laryngeal hoarseness with mucus on the vocal cords. You and I know all about it, without going to any tome of definitions. Only we probably would not include the adjective " slight." I have had to struggle all my life against such a pesky amphibian and, very sorrowfully, I observe that you have the same affliction.

The experts name several causes for these nuisances. Alcohol! Not guilty, either of us. Too much tobacco! Not guilty in my case and I think not in yours. Too much coffee! Not guilty in my case. Self-consciousness and nervousness! Alas, I must hang my head. And I suspect that right here is where your face turns scarlet.

I don't think that there is anything the matter with your throat, but I do think that there is something the matter with your mental attitude. You think too much about the spokesman and not enough about the message. You wonder whether you are going to forget your principal division or your most telling illustration. You are half convinced that you never can " get it over " to your people. You are worried and flurried. You have stage fright or rather pulpit fright.

It will do you no harm to consult your physician. Perhaps, if he gives you " something to gargle," you may gain confidence and serenity. I think, however, that what both you and I need to do is to be so eager to help those truth-hungry people, so enthusiastic for the Gospel in our custodianship and so confident in the blessing of Him who has commissioned us that we will forget all about ourselves, our throats and our other personal limitations.

Will you try? I shall continue to try.

CASE VI

About Sawing the Air

Dear Guilford:

You need a thoroughly digested theory of gesture. You need to get it established in your subconscious mind exactly what a gesture is for.

When you preached for three Sundays in Barton my best lady and I enjoyed what you had to say, but, frankly, we did not enjoy the way you said it.

On the way home one day she exclaimed, as though with no connection with anything in particular, " Arms and the Man! " " Mother," I said, " are you talking about Guilford? " She was.

I wonder how many miles of gestures you made in the course of one of those sermons. If you could have given one-tenth as many they might have added something to your delivery, but with constant "sawing the air" (Shakespeare) you exhausted every member of your congregation and you forfeited any service that your arms might have given.

I wish you would determine by careful thought just why you ever use any single gesture. It is not to exhibit your personal gracefulness, is it? It is not to give an impression of activity and enthusiasm, is it? It is not simply to relieve your nervous tension, is it? No, it is to *help convey and enforce a thought*. Nothing else!

If you have thoroughly established that fact in your inner consciousness you probably will be very sparing in your gesticulations. Constant emphasis results in no emphasis at all, just as when an emotional young lady underlines every word in her letter. From your first sentence to your last you swung, struck, crossed, reached, pointed upward, pointed downward, pointed forward. Some of the time I wished that I had a tremendous rubber band with which to restrain those tireless upper limbs.

I shall never forget what an old professor told us students about John L. Stoddard. He said, "I think that Stoddard of all men on the American platform makes the most effective use of gesture. For the most part, his arms hang gracefully at his sides; but once in a while he uses them and when he does every gesture *counts* for just what he intends."

"For what he intends"—there is another point for you. Of course, every gesture should be appropriate for the thought that is to be conveyed. Dear Guilford, I couldn't see any particular connection between your notion and your motion.

Now, what is the specific advice?

First, break yourself of your pernicious habit of unceasing gesticulation. Do this, not so much by conscious restraint while in the pulpit as by prayerful thought at home, with much practice before a mirror. Convince the real Guilford that he has power, as in God's service, to rid himself of that harmful overactivity.

Secondly, when you do make a gesture, let it come as the accompaniment and natural expression of a genuine idea. " All from the thought side," reiterated Charles W. Emerson, master orator and teacher. Let your eagerness to deliver a vital *thought* simply command your body. Do not say, " Now this is the place where I ought to point up to Heaven," or, " Right here is where I ought to shake a menacing finger at the audience." Instead, trust your intense cerebration to attend to your gestures. You may never know at the end of a sermon just what your hands have been doing, but if you are free from habit all your limbs will be good partners for your voice and your eyes.

CASE VII

The Last Man

Dear Raymond:

You write that you are much embarrassed because some of your parishioners are unable to hear your sermons. That does seem astonishing, inasmuch as you were once cheer leader at college and certainly had more than average vocal power. And I well remember hearing you call successfully from the chapel steps to a fellow away down on Berry Street. Has something happened to your equipment?

No, of course not. The reason that your pal heard you was that you adapted your voice to the distance away across the campus. You did it unconsciously, but when you thought a call to Berry Street you did adjust your voice.

Now, what is the trouble on Sunday mornings? You simply speak in a general way to the assembly and your words do not get beyond the middle of the auditorium. Or they miss some of the difficult corners.

What you ought to do is to ascertain, by careful experiments, just what sections of the church present the most trying acoustic problems. Then be sure that you include in your thought the last man. He may not be the man in the back row, for churches are peculiar. Not the most distant man, but the most difficult man is the one to be served. If he hears you need not worry about the rest of the congregation.

Prayer to Precede Self-examination

I give Thee my heartfelt thanks, God of all blessing, that Thou dost permit me to share with other needy children of Thine in the comfort and joy of Thy holy truth.

I thank Thee for the power of speech, for lips and lungs and all the physical organs by which I may transmit Thy word.

Henceforth, O Father, I desire never to neglect them and never to fail to use them to the utmost for Thy glory and for the service of men and women who need the message of power and gladness.

I consecrate my lips. I consecrate my lungs. I consecrate all my organs of speech.

SEARCHING SELF-EXAMINATION

(These questions are for no eyes but those of the minister himself. Each is to be considered thoughtfully, prayerfully and repeatedly.)

1. Do I take seriously my commission as " an angel of the Lord "?

   Answer ....

2. Do I ever take time to enumerate my organs of speech and to give earnest thanks for each one?

   Answer ....

3. Do I know that by giving thanks for each organ of speech I bring to it additional vitality and power?

   Answer ....

4. Have I heard ministers who have had " irresistible voices "?

   Answer ....

5. Do I know how those voices have been cultivated?

   Answer ....

6. Do I think that time and money spent for vocal culture are wisely invested?

   Answer ....

7. Do I believe that ministers, as much as singers or radio announcers, should care intelligently for vocal organs?

   Answer ....

8. Do I read aloud in the family circle?

   Answer ....

9. Do I take on Sunday mornings the proper nourishment in proper amounts and at proper times?

   Answer ....

10. Do I " er " and " ah "?

    Answer ....

11. Have I any similar habit that disturbs my audience and renders my speech ineffective?

    Answer ....

12. Have I a frog in my throat?

    Answer ....

13. If so, is it due to a physical cause or a psychological cause?

    Answer ....

14. What can I do to banish it?

    Answer ....

15. Do I saw the air nervously and distressingly?

    Answer ....

16. Do I consider the difference between effective gesture and senseless gesticulation?

    Answer ....

17. Is my voice too loud for the size of my auditorium?

    Answer ....

18. Is it too light?

    Answer ....

19. Do I *think* my message to the man in the most difficult section of the church?

    Answer ....

20. If I were to receive a generous financial gift would I use part of it for training in delivery?

    Answer ....

_____

After considering all the suggested points, what ought I to do?

What *will* I do?

Prayer: Help me, O Father God, to develop my powers to the utmost and always to speak as one commissioned from on High.

Section Eleven

"WHEN A FELLER'S FEELIN' BLUE"

(Several young ministers have become, for various reasons, despondent regarding themselves and their careers. Their former teacher believes that they are worth saving for the Church and endeavors, by kindly counsel, to restore hope to their minds and smiles to their faces.)

It would be thrilling if anyone could tell how many ministers old Father Harmon saved for the church, most of them excellent men with creditable careers. He was called the " pastor of the pastors." He had the knack of taking a sorry brother, deep in the doldrums, and saying just the right thing in just the right way. His prescription varied to meet the different cases, but always contained one element: Bible. One man might need financial straightening out—and Bible. Another might need homiletical counsel—and Bible. Another might need a good " raking over the coals "—and Bible. Another might need just good paternal comfort after parochial thoughtlessness and cruelty—and Bible. Always he attended conventions and always some " feller feeling blue " would get him aside for a heart-to-heart conversation. Always also a wavering apostle would go home with a new confidence and a higher consecration. On the introductory page of the volume issued in his memory was the single text: " They that be wise shall shine as the brightness of the firmament and they that turn many to righteousness as the stars forever and ever."

CASE I

Here Am I, O Lord. Send Someone Else!

Rev. Thomas C. Hopewell,
Marshall, Nebraska.

My dear Thomas:

You are scared. You are frightened about your job.

Just as I begin to write this letter I catch, by a queer coincidence, the doggerel sung by children playing out in the dooryard:

> " 'Fraid cat! 'Fraid cat!
> Don't come where I am at! "

Thomas, I must postpone for a few days a detailed consideration of your manuscripts, merely saying now that your sermons are far better than the average.

What, then, is the lack that makes you so ineffective and so unhappy? We will have to get down to psychological and spiritual facts. We will have to question your whole attitude toward your work as a preacher of the Gospel.

You distrust yourself, do you not? You dread your homiletic preparation, do you not?

I knew a man of very unusual ability, who might have gone far in his profession and who ought to have gloried in his opportunities, but who passed all through life overworried and overwearied. His wife confided to me that he was " haunted by the sermon ghost " from one week's end to the other. His study was always a place of doubt, anxiety and gloom. That was not all, however, for wherever he went the same awful obsession kept him miserable. He never could enjoy his pastoral calling, for always in the recesses of his mind was the dread thought that he had a sermon to prepare. He never felt free when reading a book, or when doing his errands, or when frolicking with the children. Constantly he seemed to hear some warning voice calling out, " What are you going to preach? What are you going to prea-ea-each? " That man grew old too fast. He never was half as successful as his powers made possible. His ministry was interrupted and practically ended by a long siege of nervous prostration, due, not to overwork, but to a failure to adjust himself to his God-given mission.

You are in danger of the same deplorable mistake. Just how glad are you to be an apostle of Christ? Mr. Spurgeon once asked a similar question of a trembling young preacher and greatly helped him by insisting upon an answer.

Thomas, are you overwhelmed with thankfulness that you are permitted to proclaim the most glorious good news that ever has entered a human mind?

The subjects of your six sermons are well chosen. " The Mind of Christ in a Twentieth Century Disciple," " Applying the Gospel in International Life," " Jesus, Still the Light of the World "—those are timely topics. " The Things of Which St. Paul Was Certain," " When Hope is Put in Harness," " The Salt that Has Not Lost Its Savor "—those are vital themes. You lack, however, spontaneity in development. I detect that your work is forced and difficult. I am willing to wager that you never rush up to your study, eager-footed, three steps at a time. You creep, like a snail, unwillingly to your desk. I now understand the troubled, almost fretful look that you wore when you were back for Commencement. You were not half enjoying the reunion, for all the while you were wondering about your sermon for the next Sunday and the next and the next.

Let me ask you if you think that worry is an aid to efficiency in lines of work other than your own. Would you like to hire a stevedore who was continually doubting that he would be able to lift the bags and boxes?

Would you like to engage a surgeon who was shackled by self-consciousness and self-distrust? Would you give your legal contest into the hands of a lawyer who continually questioned his own ability?

Self-conceit is always ridiculous, but self-respect and self-confidence are necessary preliminaries for any important success.

You, as a leader in religion, have special reasons and obligations to keep serene.

For one thing, your joy in your supreme message and ministry ought to crowd out your crippling thought of your own insufficiency. Paul said, " Woe is me if I preach not the Gospel! " and undoubtedly he would have said, " Gladness is me if I do proclaim the message of the great salvation! " John Wesley said that he was so happy in his truth that he always wanted to sing when he stood up to preach. Phillips Brooks said to a young theological student, " The older I grow and the more I think about the unrivalled privileges of my profession, the more do I pity men who are not likewise blessed." In similar spirit other men, not prominent in the eyes of the world, but gloriously content in ordinary fields, have been liberated from fear and doubt. You ought to think less of yourself and more of the troubled people whom you are commissioned to lead and enlighten, of the young fellow who has been stealing from his mother, of the merchant on the verge of bankruptcy, of the woman soul-sick with the humdrum of her existence, of the sinner self-disgusted after a moral lapse, of the husband dazed with grief over the loss of the dear home-maker. You have a great message for each one, have you not? Remember it, remember them, forget yourself.

The other reason for your confidence is that you are a man of prayer. I do not know just what your theory of petition may be; but I feel certain that you believe that by some method you may so open yourself to the abundant grace of God, may so unite yourself with the Infinite, that your wisdom may be supplemented by a wisdom higher than the human and your strength may be supplemented by a strength greater than the human. You believe that the same Father who has called you to proclaim His word and perform His work will vouchsafe the power to make possible your success.

I charge you, therefore, to get down on your knees before you begin any sermon. Yes, I mean that in a perfectly literal sense, for the physical attitude will help the spiritual attitude. Get down on your knees and ask for inspiration and reinforcement. Then remain for a long time. Remain and give enthusiastic thanks that you have received that intellectual and spiritual quickening for which you have asked and that now you are permitted to guide men and women, youths and maidens, little children, all of whom greatly need your truth. You will never make a better investment of your time. Remain until you are all aglow in mind and heart. Then rise, go with bounding steps to your study, welcome the high thoughts that come crowding for expression, and, with ease and great gladness, prepare your message of salvation.

Yours for religion in the ministry,
The Pedagogue Homiletical.

CASE II

As to Striking Twelve

Dear Ford:

Some day I'll write to you about the sermons that you have sent, but just now I'll answer the accompanying letter. Cheer up, lad. You're not the only preacher who has his days of " disgust and dismay." You say that you no longer seem to strike twelve, that four or five seems to be your highest attainment. You say that you are like a poet whose muse has deserted. You say that after church you feel like going home and hiding in some dark closet.

Go ahead and hide once or twice if you want to. Possibly in your seclusion you might get into a healthier frame of mind.

You had better remember that very few people can strike twelve every time or even many times. Young Billy came home last night, having been down to the city to attend a ball game and especially to see some leading pitcher—Feller, I believe was the name. And was he rampant! He wished he had his money back! "Rotten! Rotten!" was all he could say about Bobbie's work in the box. That doesn't mean that the young athlete ought to send in his resignation. It means that he had an off day.

Once I had the very great privilege of talking with Edwin Booth, probably the greatest actor America has produced. He confided to me that after all his years of experience and of arduous toil he sometimes had performances that seemed to him absolutely worthless. Always, he said, his work was of very uneven merit.

Ministers have off days. Of course. Sometimes the digestion is imperfect. Sometimes the church ventilation is poor. Sometimes the theme is inappropriate. Sometimes the congregation is in an unresponsive mood. And so on.

Sometimes a minister even has an off year.

Yes, I'll take up these sermons in detail. In the meantime, let me assure you that they are not worthless rubbish. You are not a hopeless ignoramus, Ford. Perhaps you are striking far higher than you think.

CASE III

Somebody Said

Dear Alvin:

Yes, they have been talking about you. You ask me

to look over your sermons and tell you what in the world
you can do to make your work as good as Dr. Westerbrook's used to be. You are in deep distress, if not
despair, because you have overheard two or three parishioners saying that they would like to listen to another
sermon by dear Dr. Westerbrook.

My advice to you is to do your own work in your own
way according to your own gifts, to put in " your best
licks," and to forget your honored predecessor.

Any minister who does not wear ear mufflers will hear,
in the course of a lifetime, a good many upsetting remarks. He may catch somebody complaining because
he seems immature or because he tries to be too " high-
brow " or because his sermons are too simple or what not
and what not. Sometimes these remarks really are made
about him and sometimes he merely thinks they are.

Once in a while a wise man may get a very valuable
suggestion from such overhearings. In other cases he
may do well to consider that chance remarks may sometimes be made quite thoughtlessly by some of his best
friends and most ardent admirers.

You know, Alvin, the old phrenologists used to talk
a great deal about " approbativeness "—definition obvious. Don't spoil your ministry by being too " approba-
tive."

CASE IV

That Awful Sermon—and a Sequel

Dear Forrest:

You say that you send the batch of sermons because
you agreed with the other boys to do so but that you do
it with reluctance, inasmuch as you are about to leave the
ministry. You declare that you are giving up your profession, not because it is a bad job, but because you are a

poor preacher. Not believing that you are simply trying to get a pat on the back, I will say that you are not so poor as you probably think. My fellow teachers have confidence that you are among our promising young men and I agree.

What has happened? You have felt for a while that your sermons have not been up to the mark. Some, according to your judgment, have been dreadful. Your people have not been so enthusiastic in thanks and congratulations as they once were.

I'll tell you a story. A minister felt that he had a bad season. In fact he was as thoroughly discouraged as you now are. One sermon in particular seemed to him to mark the depths of homiletic failure. Ten years afterward, when he went back to visit in that parish, a man said to him, "I want to thank you at this late date for your sermons during the winter when my family was broken up and my life seemed useless, and I want to tell you that that sermon of yours on 'Deep Calleth Unto Deep' probably saved me intellectually and spiritually." And that was his awful sermon! It came to him that others, as well as that distressed parishioner, had been helped during his period of depression.

We are not always good judges of our own sermons. Oftentimes, alas, we rate them too highly. Sometimes we underrate them. Forrest, don't write that letter of resignation.

CASE V

A Good Man Gone Wrong

Dear Walter:

"What *is* the trouble?" you ask. You know that your sermons are good. With disappointment, bewilderment, and resentment, you send me a few samples and ask why in the world the people do not show some appreciation. You go so far as to threaten to transfer yourself to the teaching profession, where you think you might be better recognized.

I suppose that you are thick-skinned enough to accept sweetly what I shall have to say.

The trouble is not with your sermons, Walter. They are good, almost as good, probably, as you think they are.

The fault is deeper than doctrine and deeper than homiletics.

I think that I will not talk about your own case; instead I will tell you about a man who, if he had been just slightly different, might have been the leading minister in our whole Church. Unfortunately nobody liked him. People admired him but they did not enjoy him. They were offended by his patronizing air and his over-elaborate smile. His career was ruined by over-abundant self-adulation.

Inferior men were elected to denominational offices and were called to prominent pulpits. He was disgusted. He was disgruntled. It was a sad thing, a very sad thing, for a man with such high possibilities to fail because of his condescending attitude toward less gifted associates.

I would like to be sure, Walter, that no other man of power and promise will follow him in his disappointment. Alas, that intellectual pre-eminence ever should result in apostolic catastrophe!

CASE VI

"Resignation Accepted"

Dear Elmo:

The situation is not so bad as you think. You are not so dreadful as you think.

I speak gently to you, for you are passing through one

of the most tragic and trying experiences of ministerial life. You have been asked to resign and you speak of yourself as " rejected, ejected and dejected." Your people, loving you as a pastor, but rejecting you as a preacher, have suggested " in their kindest manner " that you seek some other field.

Be thankful, Elmo, that they have done it kindly, for some other ministers, good ones too, have been dismissed very unkindly.

You send me the manuscripts because you agreed with the other fellows to do so and, you say, because you want me to see just how poor a poor sermon can be.

The trouble with you is that you take into the pulpit and thrust upon your listeners certain thoughts about yourself which, false or true, have no place in your public utterances. I dislike to say it, but you do *whine*. You make it manifest that you feel yourself to be a no-good minister, that you are indignant with those friends who induced you to essay the profession, that you wonder what is to become of you and your family, that your study has become a veritable blue grotto. You do not say all this in so many words, but you reveal it.

Just think! You preach to help people, do you not? You want to comfort them, to encourage them, to inspire them, to send them away with a new and stronger grip on the saving realities. Would these downcast sermons help anybody?

Here is your difficulty: you think that you are failing, you preach a sorrowful sermon, the people do not like it, you are sure that you are failing, you preach a more sorrowful sermon, the people like it less, and so on and so on. There you have the vicious circle.

Now you are going to a new field. Oh, yes, you are! We are not going to allow a man as good as you are to commit ministerial hara-kiri. We will see to it that you have a new place, quite comfortably distant from your present field. Then we shall demand that you do your work manfully, with no juvenile bewailments about your own deficiencies or anything else. Try, not a vicious circle, but a virtuous circle. And we, your true friends at the old school, will be cheering for you.

Oh, by the way, these sermons have many excellencies. I'll write again and specify.

CASE VII

Read the Parable of the Talents

Dear Zenas:

In your letter you mention three classmates, all of whom appear to be going high in the ministry. You say, " Look my stuff over, if you are willing, but you will not find it like the sermons of Williams, Burdett and Steiner."

No. Moreover, there is little resemblance between the work of any two of those men.

I hope that you are not going to sink into jealousy and envy. I hope that you are not going to develop a fatal self-depreciation. If other men are doing excellent work in their pulpits, rejoice exceedingly, inasmuch as they are helping to bring in the Kingdom.

Your own privilege is to do your duty, where God has placed you, and to do it with the utmost efficiency. If you are temporarily, or even permanently, in a small field, do your best and don't worry. My own expectation in your case is that, being " faithful over a few things you will be made ruler over many."

Cheer up!

CASE VIII

De Profundis

Dear Harold:

I thank you for sending me the sermons for my sym-

pathetic attention. I thank you also for honoring me
with the very confidential note. I do not know what to
say to you about your very serious transgression, for it
is not for me either to condemn or condone. I am glad,
however, that you feel so thoroughly wretched over the
whole affair, inasmuch as that leads me to believe that
you have had a lapse and not a collapse.

I do not think that our church leaders would wish you
to " pack up and start for Australia " or to inflict any
other self-castigation that would mean the abandonment
of your career.

Advise yourself as you would advise another young
man in similar circumstances. Repent with all your
might. Pray so earnestly that there will be no danger
of a repetition of your sin. Then let all your preaching
be richer, sweeter, more tolerant, more Christian, because
you can understand something of the soul crises that come
to other imperfect human beings.

I commend to you quite frequent readings of a little
poem written by one of our professors and called, " The
True Repentance ":

> " Hast thou sinned and is there creeping
> O'er thy soul the sense of blight?
> Art thou now the whirlwind reaping?
> Does remorse make all seem night?

> " Spend no time in idle weeping
> While thy *work* awaits thy might,
> For the penance worth the keeping
> Profits all within thy sight."

PRAYER TO PRECEDE SELF-EXAMINATION

*O God, who dost deign to allow Thy human children
to be fellow laborers with Thee, I thank Thee that Thou
hast called me to speak the Gospel of power and patience
and peace. Help me to set an example of faith and faith-*

fulness. May I not be discouraged by the inevitable difficulties and disappointments of Christian service.

Deliver me from false pride and personal aggrandizement.

Help me to be single of heart and persistent in endeavor.

May I regard each failure as a challenge to better work and each success as an invitation to larger enterprise.

SEARCHING SELF-EXAMINATION

(These questions are for no eyes but those of the minister himself. Each is to be considered thoughtfully, prayerfully and repeatedly.)

1. Am I habitually unhappy and despondent about my preaching?

   Answer ....

2. Do I approach my homiletic task with doubt and dread?

   Answer ....

3. Am I haunted by " the sermon ghost "?

   Answer ....

4. Am I as grateful as I ought to be for the privilege of proclaiming the great good news?

   Answer ....

5. Do I worry myself into inefficiency?

   Answer ....

6. Do I worry myself into physical illness?

   Answer ....

7. Do I forget that when I do His work God is on my side?

   Answer ....

8. Do I pray with confidence about my preaching?

Answer ....

9. Am I discouraged if in some sermons I am not at my best?

Answer ....

10. Am I tempted quite often to write my resignation?

Answer ....

11. Am I tempted quite often to quit the ministry?

Answer ....

12. Am I too much affected by what I overhear or think I overhear about myself?

Answer ....

13. Do I feel that lack of praise implies lack of appreciation?

Answer ....

14. Do I whine?

Answer ....

15. Do I forget the apostolic injunction not to think of myself more highly than I ought to think?

Answer ....

16. Have I a complex that ought to be removed by earnest prayer?

Answer ....

17. Do I make myself miserable by comparing myself with men seemingly more successful?

Answer ....

18. Do I feel that others are unjustly promoted in my stead?

Answer ....

19. Do I apply the Parable of the Talents to the work of the Christian ministry?

Answer ....

20. Do I preach for my own glory or for the service of God?

Answer ....

After considering all the suggested points, what ought I to do?

What *will* I do?

Prayer: Dear God, help me to work thankfully in fields great or small according to Thy will. Help me " if I may never do a great thing to do many small things in a great spirit."

SECTION TWELVE

" HERE I STAND. I CAN DO NO OTHERWISE "

(The veteran minister is grieved by the pusillanimous tone of some of the sermons that former students have sent to him for criticism. He feels that some young preachers of today need to develop the spirit of Martin Luther and John Knox.)

WHEN, in Edinburgh, you walk " the royal mile " from the palace to the castle you are likely to step upon a brass disk set in the roadway, set there with hatred so that everybody may tread upon it. It bears the initials " I.

K.," equivalent to " J. K.," and marks the grave of John Knox.

There was a man who never dodged issues or minced words.

When Thomas Carlyle looked at that disk he said, " There lies the body of a man who never feared the face of any human being."

CASE I

Nothing in Particular

Classroom Number 6

Rev. Theodore Harper,
Richford, Georgia.

My dear Theodore:

There is a minister, well known to both you and me, who has the physique of a giant, the face of a philosopher, the voice of a prophet—and the vocabulary of a nice young poetess. He is a past master in the art of saying nothing in beautiful phrases and graceful figures of speech. With marvellous skill he avoids assuming responsibility on any issue. He loves tact, but eschews fact. He makes no enemies—and no converts. Theodore, beware of his sad example. Waste not your life in charming euphemism. Say something. Stand for something. Be somebody.

When you spoke at the Chicago convention, having been assigned the pregnant theme of " An Outreaching Christianity," your friends thought that your great opportunity had come, an opportunity to deliver a striking and helpful message and at the same time to demonstrate before important people that you were a man of power and promise. Frankly, we were disappointed. Your language was exalted, but your thought was vague. You convinced nobody, because you revealed no conviction.

You hit no mark, because you gave the impression that you had none. President Collins spoke to me about you later in the afternoon. He said, "If your *protégé* plays golf with as much precision as he speaks in public, he must get a score of about five hundred." Don't be offended at Prexy, who is your friend, and who, in a spirit of helpfulness, has given me permission to quote his words. Take him seriously.

When I received your six sermons with a request for candid criticism, I hoped to find that your Chicago utterance had been exceptional. I looked, in these samples from your regular ministry, for strong, virile expression, thought-compelling and character-influencing. I am forced to say, however, that you sent me a half dozen servings of what the theologues call " eloquent mush." You have heard the old story of the pussyfooting preacher who told his people that they must " repent (er-r-r so to speak) and be baptized (er-r-r as it were) or be damned (er-r-r to a certain extent)." Imitate him not.

First from your batch I read your sermon for Armistice Day. It's long enough. It must have taken you thirty-five or forty minutes to dodge all the issues that came to your mind. You had much to say about the glories of war and you had much to say also about the beauties of peace, but I declare I cannot understand which side of any question you are on. Perhaps you had some militarists in your congregation and so, for their comfort, you became almost a militarist; and perhaps you had some pacifists and so, to please them, you became almost a pacifist. Some of the saddest tragedies of life center around people who " almost " amount to something.

I proceeded to read " A Creed for the Twentieth Century " and I was chiefly impressed with the thought that you did not intend to arouse opposition from any quarter. So with the others: " Now that Election is Over," " A Christian Christmas," " What to Do with the New Year," and " Re-Thinking Missions." I appreciate your evident industry. Throughout every discourse, however, I kept repeating, " Oh, why doesn't he say something! "

Here are your constantly recurring expressions: " It possibly may be," " It has been said by some," " Probably," " It might seem," " Some may think." What do *you* think?

Then think of your euphemisms. Instead of sin you speak of " disregard of usually accepted canons of deportment." Instead of drunkenness you say " unfortunate indulgence in the liquor that inebriates." Instead of political corruption you say " less than highest conception of patriotism." If a man should strike you in the face would you say that he showed less than the highest conception of courtesy?

I have been trying to decide just what psychological and spiritual effect such rhetorical side-stepping must have on ordinary hearers. There is danger of four undesirable verdicts.

Some people may say, " He's a Miss Nancy." They want a real man in the pulpit. They look for vigor in thought and expression. They enjoy beauty and poetry, but only such as are consistent with masculine personality.

Others may say, " He's an intellectual shirk." They want a positive message from one who has forced himself to think through to conclusions and convictions. They know that often it is easier to invent an ornate figure of speech than to follow an involved argument.

Some listeners may say, " He's a coward." They are suspicious of a man who coats his pill with too much sugar. They do not demand someone who agrees with them on every point, someone who simply holds up the mirror of their own minds. They despise a preacher who is one of the

" Slaves who fear to speak
For the fallen and the weak."

And a fourth class of hearers may say, "He's an empty-head." They may say, "He dilutes because he has little in his mind." They may suppose that he tries to make up for paucity of thought by fecundity of words. They look for important ideas definitely and concisely expressed.

I do not mean that the members of your congregation necessarily put these verdicts into oral or written form. I do mean that they may carry them in the back of their minds and from them may form their general estimate of their minister.

Now, for some reason you have been changing since your college days, when you used to be upright and outright and forthright. Resist your tendency, for I warn you that dodging an issue leads not only to poor literary style but to serious moral degeneration.

What can you do? I advise you to read the sermons of some of the outstanding preachers of the country, men of recognized influence. See how they declare themselves. No beating around the bush! No exaggerated caution! No hesitation to call a spade a spade! They say many things that you do not like, but they always keep your respect.

Once in your study I saw the photograph of old Doctor Bentham, heroic pastor and preacher in our local church during your college days. Take him for an ideal. When you are preparing a sermon, look up at that picture and imagine with what spirit that sturdy old saint would have declared himself. I am not suggesting that you try to imitate his inimitable literary style, for that would be silly and futile. What I do mean is that you may well seek to cultivate his spirit of unflinching advocacy of right and outspoken opposition of wrong. Remember how you boys used to say, "We do not always agree with 'Old Father,' but we always know where he stands."

Theodore, get out your *Sartor Resartus*. Read it every

day and let it fire your soul. Then say something in particular, and fear not.

Yours for the Kingdom that is to come,
The Pedagogue Homiletical.

CASE II

"What a Piece of Work is a Man!"

Dear Hugh:

I always like the name "Hugh." It has a rugged strength that gives me a sense of support and safety. It has stood for great character in human history.

You have a masculine name and you have a masculine frame, seventy-two inches in height. You shave every morning, at least you ought to, for you have a beard. Your voice is deep.

Oh, dear, I wish your sermons were as masculine as your personality!

We have some women in our ministry. That's all right. They should, however, be womanly women and not manly women.

And our men should be manly men, not womanly men.

I wish you would talk less about the pretty little things of life and more about the tremendous things. "Violets!" "Birdlets!" "Rivulets!" Somehow, they do not seem in keeping with your big, masculine selfhood.

I do not mean that you ought not to "commune with Nature in her visible forms." I think, though, that you ought to express your reactions a little differently from the way in which Sister Susie would.

And I have regretted that in all the six sermons you have sent me I find no serious reference to the unprecedented problems with which the world is now perplexed, no protest against arrant and aggressive evil and no clarion call for outspoken, sacrificial Christian citizenship.

CASE III

The Voice of the Church

Dear Lyndon:

It is a thrilling honor that we ministers have received, that of being spokesmen for the Christian Church, and it is a heavy responsibility that we carry. To think that the Church of Jesus Christ, a Church now on trial before humanity, should be judged by what we say and how we say it! It is no wonder that we are appalled.

I wish your sermons might reveal a fuller awareness of this twentieth-century crisis and a firmer position in regard to Christian service.

I cannot see much to criticize in these manuscripts, but, oh, your subjects do seem inconsequential at a time like this. What are you reading these days? What are you thinking?

I wonder if these irrelevant and inadequate sermons are typical of those that are going out of our American pulpits. I wonder!

Is it possible that the Church is just doubtfully following on while leadership is being taken over by men and women outside its folds? The other day two victuallers went through the train upon which I was riding. The first was an imposing fellow who called out in a car-filling voice, ''*S A N D W I C H E S !   S A N D - W I C H E S !*'' Then, almost obscured, followed a tiny specimen of humanity who weakly piped, "And coffee! And coffee!"

I hope that in the struggle for honesty and purity and fair play the Christian Church is going to lead and not tremblingly follow. And I hope that you boys from my classroom are going to be courageous pioneers.

CASE IV

Pussy Foote

Dear Ashley:

No one would think of giving your brother Albert such a nickname, or your cousin Gilbert. They are both Footes, but one is called " Doc " and the other is called " Baron." Those are terms of respect and affection, but I am afraid that your nickname, " Pussy," is a term of distrust.

At school I never knew you to take a decided stand on any question. Trying to be on all sides at once, you were on no particular side. Endeavoring to be friends with all parties, you were friend of none.

Alas, your sermons reveal no change. There is nothing stalwart about them. You are on the fence every time. You make me think of Bill Nye, who said that some people had such " balanced minds " that they were ready to turn in one direction or the other, according to the slightest wind.

I wish you wouldn't side-step. I wish you wouldn't straddle. I wish you wouldn't mince matters. I wish you wouldn't pussy-foot.

Then your sermons, excellent in form and language, would be worth preaching.

CASE V

The Artful Dodger

Dear Bruce:

I am going to violate one of my strictest rules. I have said that I will never repeat to a person what I hear said about him, but I am going to tell you what a certain member of your congregation called you. It will hurt you. Take it in the right spirit. Don't be over-angry at him or at me.

He said, " Our minister is the artful dodger." That was pretty bad. He continued, " Our minister never really declares himself on any controversial subject; about pacifism, for instance, or about the liquor question, or about our denominational government. He seems to think that if he spoke out like a man he would offend somebody. As a matter of fact, he offends us all by his hedging and dodging."

I thought this man was overstating the case and I told him so. Now, however, I have read your sermons and I am forced to think that he is right. So—just as I was trying to think what more to say to you the poem by Maltbie D. Babcock came ringing in my ears. Babcock, my personal friend, was a great man. I think he would like to have me quote his great challenge for your benefit.

> " Be strong!
> We are not here to play, to dream, to drift.
> We have hard work to do and loads to lift.
> Shun not the struggle—face it; 'tis God's gift.
>
> " Be strong!
> Say not the days are evil. Who's to blame?
> And fold the hands and acquiesce.—O shame!
> Stand up, speak out, and bravely, in God's name.
>
> " Be strong!
> It matters not how deep intrenched the wrong,
> How hard the battle goes, the day how long;
> Faint not—fight on! Tomorrow comes the song! "

CASE VI

Hard Fact and Soft Language

Dear Percival:

There are times when it is not necessary for a gentleman to be gentle in his language. There are periods (and this is one of them) when a Christian minister ought to make manifest his righteous indignation.

1 see that your sermons deal considerably with the great evils that confront our American society and that have permeated the life of your own community. That is good so far as it goes.

But do you speak harshly enough? Do you hit hard enough? I regret your apparent half relenting and half consenting.

Do you know what Mrs. Phillips said to her son Wendell, when he started out on his crusade against human slavery? She said, " Wendell, don't shilly-shally." And he never did.

PRAYER TO PRECEDE SELF-EXAMINATION

O Thou, who hast given me my great commission, help me to be a good soldier of Jesus Christ.

Help me to fight the good fight, to finish my course, to keep the faith.

May I never fear to speak the truth.

SEARCHING SELF-EXAMINATION

(These questions are for no eyes but those of the minister himself. Each is to be considered thoughtfully, prayerfully and repeatedly.)

1. Am I positive in thought and pulpit personality?

   Answer ....

2. Is my language more poetic than powerful?

   Answer ....

3. Is there any danger that people will consider me a womanly man?

   Answer ....

4. Does anyone ever call me a " Miss Nancy "?

Answer ....

5. If I am not satisfactorily masculine in thought and manner, how can I improve myself in that respect?

Answer ....

6. Do I realize that the Christian Church is being judged by the virility of its preachers?

Answer ....

7. Would I be pleased and proud to have the Christian Church judged by my virility?

Answer ....

8. Do I ever say nothing in beautiful phrases?

Answer ....

9. Are my statements so clear that no one can mistake my stand on important issues?

Answer ....

10. Have I the courage of my convictions?

Answer ....

11. Do I make undue use of euphemisms?

Answer ....

12. Could anyone ever suspect me of being an " artful dodger "?

Answer ....

13. Do I ever manifest righteous indignation against the great evils of the times?

Answer ....

14. Am I a student of applied Christianity?

Answer ....

15. Am I afraid of my trustees?

Answer ....

16. Would I obey my church officers rather than my conscience?

Answer ....

17. Am I afraid of the local newspapers?

Answer ....

18. What are the outstanding evils of my own community?

Answer ....

19. Am I unpopular with the gamblers, liquor dealers and profiteers in vice?

Answer ....

20. If I should leave my church would it be a great blow to the moral life of the community?

Answer ....

_____

After considering all the suggested points, what ought I to do?

What *will* I do?

Prayer: *God of all Power, through whose service comes high success, strengthen my faith, strengthen my heart, strengthen my eagerness to proclaim Thy truth.*

CONCLUSION

A HUNDRED years ago a minister kept a diary. He was a pioneer preacher in New York State, his duties requiring him to preach at least three times every Sunday and often between Sundays, to ride long distances on horseback, to visit all sorts of people under all sorts of conditions, to eat and sleep " when possible." His journal is now in the library of a well-known theological seminary. Day after day he closed his memoranda with the sentence, " I am very tired but very glad."